MODELING IN URBAN AND REGIONAL ECONOMICS

FUNDAMENTALS OF PURE AND APPLIED ECONOMICS

EDITORS IN CHIEF

J. LESOURNE, Conservatoire National des Arts et Métiers, Paris, France
H. SONNENSCHEIN, University of Pennsylvania, Philadelphia, PA, USA

ADVISORY BOARD

REGIONAL & URBAN ECONOMICS II
In 4 Volumes

MODELING IN URBAN AND REGIONAL ECONOMICS

ALEX ANAS

ROUTLEDGE
Taylor & Francis Group

First published in 1987 by
Harwood Academic Publishers GmbH

Reprinted in 2001 by
Routledge
2 Park Square, Milton Park, Abingdon, Oxon, OX14 4RN

Transferred to Digital Printing 2007

Routledge is an imprint of the Taylor & Francis Group

© 1987 Harwood Academic Publishers GmbH

The publishers have made every effort to contact authors/copyright holders
of the works reprinted in *Harwood Fundamentals of Pure & Applied Economics*.
This has not been possible in every case, however, and we would welcome
correspondence from those individuals/companies we have been unable to
trace.

These reprints are taken from original copies of each book. in many cases
the condition of these originals is not perfect. the publisher has gone to
great lengths to ensure the quality of these reprints, but wishes to point
out that certain characteristics of the original copies will, of necessity, be
apparent in reprints thereof.

British Library Cataloguing in Publication Data
A CIP catalogue record for this book
is available from the British Library

Modeling in Urban and Regional Economics
ISBN 0-415-26973-3
Regional & Urban Economics II: 4 Volumes
ISBN 0-415-26972-5
Harwood Fundamentals of Pure & Applied Economics
ISBN 0-415-26907-5

Modeling in Urban and Regional Economics

Alex Anas
Northwestern University, USA

A volume in the Regional and Urban Economics section

edited by

Richard Arnott
Queen's University, Canada

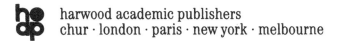 harwood academic publishers
chur · london · paris · new york · melbourne

© 1987 by Harwood Academic Publishers GmbH
Poststrasse 22, 7000 Chur, Switzerland
All rights reserved

Harwood Academic Publishers

Post Office Box 197
London WC2E 9PX
England

58, rue Lhomond
75005 Paris
France

Post Office Box 786
Cooper Station
New York, NY 10276
United States of America

Private Bag 8
Camberwell, Victoria 3124
Australia

Library of Congress Cataloging-in-Publication Data

Anas, Alex.
    Modeling in urban and regional economics.

    (Fundamentals of pure and applied economics,
ISSN 0191-1708; vol. 26. Regional and urban economics section)
    Bibliography: p.
    Includes index.
    1. Urban economics—Mathematical models. 2. Regional economics—
Mathematical models. I. Title. II. Series: Fundamentals of pure and applied
economics; vol. 26. III. Series: Fundamentals of pure and applied economics.
Regional and urban economics section.
HT321.A52   1987   330'.0724   87-27518
ISBN 3-7186-0467-1

Contents

Introduction to the Series

Drawing on a personal network, an economist can still relatively easily stay well informed in the narrow field in which he works, but to keep up with the development of economics as a whole is a much more formidable challenge. Economists are confronted with difficulties associated with the rapid development of their discipline. There is a risk of "balkanisation" in economics, which may not be favorable to its development.

Fundamentals of Pure and Applied Economics has been created to meet this problem. The discipline of economics has been subdivided into sections (listed inside). These sections include short books, each surveying the state of the art in a given area.

Each book starts with the basic elements and goes as far as the most advanced results. Each should be useful to professors needing material for lectures, to graduate students looking for a global view of a particular subject, to professional economists wishing to keep up with the development of their science, and to researchers seeking convenient information on questions that incidentally appear in their work.

Each book is thus a presentation of the state of the art in a particular field rather than a step-by-step analysis of the development of the literature. Each is a high-level presentation but accessible to anyone with a solid background in economics, whether engaged in business, government, international organizations, teaching, or research in related fields.

Three aspects of *Fundamentals of Pure and Applied Economics* should be emphasized:

—First, the project covers the whole field of economics, not only theoretical or mathematical economics.

—Second, the project is open-ended and the number of books is not predetermined. If new interesting areas appear, they will generate additional books.

—Last, all the books making up each section will later be grouped to constitute one or several volumes of an Encyclopedia of Economics.

The editors of the sections are outstanding economists who have selected as authors for the series some of the finest specialists in the world.

J. Lesourne   *H. Sonnenschein*

Modeling in Urban and Regional Economics

ALEX ANAS

Northwestern University, Evanston, Illinois, USA

INTRODUCTION

Ideally, the development of a science follows a three-phase progression. The first phase is the formulation of theory. The second phase is the empirical testing of specific models which stem from the theory and the third phase is the application of the science to real problems. In the natural sciences, application is achieved by the creation of technology. In the social sciences, and in economics in particular, application consists of building a mathematical model capable of making predictions (or forecasts) of markets and able to analyze, evaluate and determine selected public decisions and aspects of public policy.

It is rare that the ideal progression described above occurs in just that way. Often, empirical models with little theoretical grounding are developed and applied in advance of the birth of a theory. Such activity can highlight and stimulate the arrival of the theory. Empirical work and application following a theory often leads to revised and more mature statements of the theory which then lead to additional rounds of testing and application.

It is also possible that application can occur without any prior theory or at least no prior empirical testing of a theory. Ships were invented much before Archimedes formulated his law of buoyancy and the Wright brothers could fly with only a rudimentary and poorly tested theory of aerodynamics. Similarly, in the social sciences a qualitatively formulated theory can inspire a jump to actual policy application or at least to practical decision making

1

without any quantitative empirical testing of the theory or the development of models based on the theory.

In urban and regional economics the interplay among theory, empirical testing and application has been particularly interesting. In urban economics, forecasting and policy analytic tools emerged in the 1960's independently from the urban economic theory which was also being formulated at that time. Since then, theoretical urban economics has achieved maturity while empirical testing and application has remained separate and has lagged somewhat behind but has been growing and converging to the theory while shaking itself loose from the early non-economic influences.

In regional economics the trends have been less confirming of the "ideal progression." Forecasting and policy oriented applied tools date back to the birth of input–output models in the early 1950's. A formal theory of the regional and interregional economy has not yet been formulated, although there is a number of hypotheses and propositions that have found empirical testing.

In this volume we are concerned not only with theoretical formulations, but with those models which belong in the realm of numerical exploration, empirical testing and policy applications of the theory. In urban and regional economics, this realm is quite broad and covers a variety of modeling styles and purposes. These will be gathered under the term "urban and regional economic modeling" or "simulation models," since all of them are numerically computable paradigmatic characterizations of the underlying reality, albeit at very different levels of simplication or empirical detail.

Five classes or types of models are identified and discussed in this volume. The fifth class contains an evaluation of the approaches that have been used in regional and interregional modeling, while the first four classes deal with urban modeling. These are "monocentric models," "non-economic models," "mathematical programming models" and "econometric models." Because the literature surveyed within each class varies considerably in its mix of theory versus application and in the qualitative versus quantitative orientation of the models, a general set of criteria that can be applied to all four classes are difficult to determine. The discussion below, therefore, is aimed at identifying each type of model and suggesting the considerations which are relevant for an evaluation.

The first breed of models deals with the numerical solution of a theoretical model the analytical solution of which has proven intractable. Simulation has been used to obtain magnitudes when explicit analytical solution is not possible and also to determine the direction of change when the comparative statics are ambiguous. In such cases the model being solved is essentially a simplified and idealized representation of reality. In urban economics, for example, the theory has been developed in the context of the, so called, nineteenth century style city with nearly all employment concentrated within a core extending a few miles around a central port or rail terminal. Housing is then assumed to be located in a circular suburban ring around the central core. Placing this idealized urban form on a featureless plain, on which transportation in any direction is equally costly, results in a one-dimensional representation in which distance from the center is the only variable which distinguishes locations. In urban economics this one-dimensional representation has come to be known as the *monocentric* model (i.e. a model with a *single employment center*). The role of "distance from the center" in a monocentric model has been compared to the role of the variable "time" in simple models of neoclassical growth theory (see [129]). In some respects, the mathematics employed to solve these two classes of models is in fact the same or very similar.

The monocentric model is a minimal model of an urban economy in the sense that it encapsulates the minimum amount of detail necessary to introduce the concept of location. As such, the monocentric model has served as a powerful parsimonious framework for building theory. Simple monocentric models have been solved analytically allowing full qualitative characterization of the solution space without any need for numerical explorations of it. The standard case capable of such solution is the long run equilibrium of land use in the suburban residential ring. For this partial equilibrium case, a full comparative static analysis has been possible (see [176, 77, 136]). Our ability to obtain full analytical solutions quickly diminishes with the introduction of additional complexity into the standard monocentric model. Some of these complexities are: (a) several classes of households which differ in preferences (utility functions), (b) presence of an externality such as traffic congestion, (c) general equilibrium versions encompassing several sectors such as production in the core, housing production in the suburban ring, transportation etc. (d) several employment locations, (e) effects of policy instruments such as the property tax.

The need to resort to numerical simulation to investigate some of these problems was recognized in 'the early seventies. This quickly gave rise to a style of analysis in which it became routine to select certain specialized functional forms and representative coefficient values and then proceed to obtain specific solutions. Despite some efforts to provide an empirical basis for the selected coefficients, the justification for this type of simulation is theoretical. In most cases the investigators used simulation to build qualitative results in a monocentric context, rather than claim more general empirical discovery. There has been, however, a tendency to draw broad-brush empirical generalizations. In some cases such attempts have been convincing, pointing the way for more realistic and larger scale empirical studies of the underlying questions.

There are, of course, some difficulties with this simulation style. An attempt to generalize results must be supported by tedious sensitivity testing whereby coefficient values are varied systematically. This is not only difficult to perform but also cumbersome to report in published form reducing the ability of the investigators to confirm and reproduce each others' results. These difficulties have been potentially mitigated by the development of numerical solution algorithms applicable to monocentric simulations (see [100, 101, 116, 117, 141, 142]). However, the actual application of these algorithms has been rather limited, perhaps because interest in monocentric models has declined toward the early eighties. Also, the numerical solution of these models still requires a lot of work because canned numerical algorithms are not available. Finally, since such models are not realistic they are used primarily to develop theoretical insight. But most theorists prefer to do purely theoretical work. They consider, not always wisely, that simulation is a poor substitute for theory. In part one of this article, we survey the problems examined by means of monocentric simulation and the contributions thus made to theoretical understanding on the one hand and to empirical discovery on the other.

The second type of applied research refers to a genre of large scale urban development models applicable on the computer. These are surveyed in part two of this article. These models are dissimilar.

They share only the following characteristics: (a) they are developed independently of urban economic theory but emerged at about the same period in time, (b) not only are these models non-economic, they are also atheoretical bearing no link or very tenuous links to *any* established theoretical framework, (c) they are intended for large scale implementation on the computer, and (d) they are tools designed to make forecasts and thus indirectly aid in the evaluation of public investment decisions or planning alternatives.

The last two characteristics explain *why* these models emerged at the time that they did. First, the use of computer based models had grown rapidly in all branches of science since the 1950's. A nearly thousand-fold decline in the real cost of computer services and the proliferation of hardware encouraged these developments. Second, the importance of prediction and forecasting became increasingly recognized by urban planners, after about a decade of experience in the narrower field of transportation planning and nearly two decades of experience with national, regional and interregional input–output tables. It was the time to build an equivalent technology for forecasting urban development. Britton Harris was at that time, and has been since then, an eloquent articulator of this need for urban development models (see [71, 72]). While the relevance of economics to this effort was understood and recognized, urban economic theory was just being born and its potential contribution to the effort appeared too elusive or remained completely unnoticed. At the same time, the need for large scale forecasting models applicable on the computer was too urgent. Thus came the models of Forrester [56], Hill [84] and Lowry [115]. Somewhat in the wake of some of these practical developments Wilson [185] proposed a statistical theory of spatial interactions encompassing the Lowry-type models which were continuing to flourish in many applications. The development of these non-economic but operational models has been a mixed blessing for urban economics. These models broke new ground pointing out, for future economic models, the major features and problems in large scale forecasting. By short circuiting the development of theory, these models have become entrenched technology that needed refinement, revamping or dislodging in the future. The chief contribution of these models has been to create new knowledge about the use of models, about computational complexity and about the limits of computers. Much has also been learned about how to represent the urban system at highly detailed levels of disaggregation. Little has accrued in substantive theoretical or empirical findings which were not already known or, in due time, became learned from the monocentric literature. Yet these models continue to be important in applications and their presence remains a challenge for urban economics.

The creators of these models did not utilize microeconomic principles in specifying the models' equations. Nevertheless, the Lowry–Wilson type spatial allocation models are built from equations which embody certain discrete substitution relationships. These types of models are now known to be very akin to stochastic discrete choice models in econometrics contributed by McFadden's [121, 122] work. Thus, the process of the careful econometric respecification of the Lowry–Wilson type models has now begun to attract attention.

The third type of simulation modeling refers to a genre of mathematical programming models intended to determine efficient land use or activity allocation in metropolitan areas. These are surveyed in part three of this article. The early theoretical work inspired the development of the Herbert and Stevens [83] linear programming model which was seen as a large scale operations research version of the market equilibrium (without market failure) formulated in the standard monocentric context. The second generation monocentric models inspired another general equilibrium model developed by Mills [124] and extended by Hartwick and Hartwick [76]. These linear programming models which are direct descendants of the simple theoretical models continue to be of applied interest. In the 1960's there were efforts to apply the Herbert and Stevens model in town planning and currently there are efforts to implement the extensions of the Mills–Hartwick models empirically. The models of Beckmann *et al.* [31] and Koopmans and Beckmann [105] predate the advent of urban economics. The former, a mathematical programming formulation for computing a traffic equilibrium on a road network has found extensive application and refinement within transportation planning, the most routinized branch of urban planning, despite its heroic and generally inconsistent assumptions of steady state traffic flow. The Koopmans–Beckmann model became the subject of a somewhat inconclusive debate regarding its implications for market failure when lumpy or indivisible investments are concerned. The development of mathematical programming models in the future could be a major focus within urban economics which, in this way, can achieve its natural role as the basic science for normative urban planning.

The fourth class of applications refers to a number of large scale, prediction oriented econometric models surveyed in part four. These models are similar to the second class with the difference that model equations are firmly rooted in urban economic theory and are in principle, if not always in practice, estimable with actual data and well understood econometric techniques. The Urban Institute Model [42] and the National Bureau of Economic Research Model [88] are two such models designed to predict the clearing of the urban housing market and the analysis of housing policy. The Chicago Area Transportation-land Use Analysis System [6] is designed as a bridge between transportation planning and urban economics: it predicts the impact of transportation changes on travel demand, housing and land prices, and on residential land development. The last two models are dynamic. In addition to these practical models which deal with one or two sectors, there has also been an inconclusive attempt to develop an econometric model of an entire metropolitan economy (see [50]). The quality of data, econometric rigor and actual application of the above models is quite nonuniform and, in some cases, rather incompletely documented. It appears, however, that future extensions of these predictive econometric models stand a good chance of gradually replacing their noneconomic counterparts currently used in planning and policy analysis.

Unlike urban economics, regional economics is not endowed with a simple and powerful formal theory equivalent to that of the "monocenric model." If such a theory were to be developed it would encompass the location, production, employment and trade decisions of firms simultaneously with the decisions of households to migrate and choose employment in an interregional economy. Differences in the economic activity profiles of various regions would be determined by differences in the stocks of natural resources, in the presence of local amenities and in the locations of the regions. Perhaps ironically, but certainly in a very logical development, urban economists in recent years have begun very slowly to extend their theory of the monocentric city to build a theory of monocentric city systems (see [80, 82]). In this way, a rudimentary framework for analyzing the regional and interregional economy has begun to emerge, shifting the emphasis from "regions" to city systems. Much remains to be done to extend this theory of city systems to incorporate explicitly economies of scale, interindustry trade and agglomeration effects and dynamics.

While "regional economic theory" may be pregnant with such developments, "regional and interregional simulation models" (the fifth use of the term simulation) predate even the birth of urban economic theory. A convenient and significant point in time is Leontieff's study of the national economy by means of the input–output table [109]. Input–output models have since then become the focus of enormous research efforts and expenditures and were rapidly adapted to the regional and interregional context by Isard [89, 90]. The economic content of input–output models is very rudimentary. The assumptions of these models do such violence to economic theory that it would be difficult to classify these models as economic were it not for their development and intensive use *by* economists over three decades. The use of input–output models is also closely associated with the use of the economic base models employed in many regional studies. Economic base and input–output approaches are essentially macroeconomic rather than microeconomic, although input–output owes its popularity to the fact that it can be applied at detailed levels of disaggregation despite its macro character.

A partial response to the lack of good economic theory in input–output models came from the development of econometric models stemming largely from the pioneering work of Klein [102] which appeared at about the same time as Leontieff's contribution. At the level of the national economy, this work has led to forecasting models such as the Wharton Annual and Long-Term Econometric Model while at the regional level the work of Glickman [65, 66] has been instrumental in establishing and testing similar models. The regional econometric models are superior to input–output techniques in the use of econometrics to estimate equations consistently and to specify them in a flexible way. Still, these techniques are also essentially macroeconomic. Urban economics has succeeded in completing the progression from a microeconomic theory to the development of applied simulation models closely linked to this microeconomic theory. Regional economics has yet to return to square one of microeconomic theory from where a new generation of applied models can be originated. The wealth of data, empirical and practical experience accumulated in the development of input–output and econometric models will undoubtedly be of value in such future developments. The literature on regional and interregional simulation models is briefly discussed in part five of this survey.

1. MONOCENTRIC MODELS

In this section we will examine the application of simulation to a number of themes in monocentric analysis. Each theme represents an area of policy or scientific interest in which prior analytical exploration quickly reached its limits and thus the application of simulation was warranted. In reviewing these themes, we will indicate why analytical investigation failed in answering the key questions and thus why numerical simulation was necessary. We will focus on what was learned from the simulations and to what extent the new knowledge enriched our understanding of reality and our insight into important policy questions. Monocentric analysis has done well to illustrate the complementarity between theory and simulation: pondering simulation results has yielded insights and generated hypotheses that stimulated theoretical develoments. We will also consider the quality of the artificial or empirical data used in the simulations, although in most cases little confidence can be placed in these data. Finally, we will examine the literature on computational methods for solving general equilibrium monocentric models. This literature emerged in the mid seventies in response to the growing trend toward numerical solutions at that time.

1.1. Income and urban location

An important result in monocentric theory is the location of different income groups within the suburban ring. Beckmann [29] examined this problem under the assumption that all households, regardless of income, had the same Cobb–Douglas utility function defined over a composite commodity purchased at the center and the size of their land plots purchased at their residential location. He also assumed that all households, regardless of income, faced the same transport cost function. The income distribution was a continuous function: the Pareto distribution. The analytically obtained result was simply that at equilibrium a household's distance from the center increased with the household's income. In 1974, Wheaton [176] formalized the well understood comparative statics of a monocentric city with a single income group and absentee landlords, and Hartwick, Schweizer and Varaiya [77] generalized Wheaton's analysis to a monocentric city with a given number of households in each income group. All income groups had different but predetermined incomes and the same utility function (defined over the composite commodity and lot size). A significant but very plausible restriction on the utility function was that land was a normal good. Under these assumptions, the authors showed that the distance of a household's ring from the center increases as the household's income increases regardless of the precise income distribution. Furthermore, they performed a full comparative static analysis examining the effect of exogenous changes on the relative welfare and land consumption of the households. An important result in this respect is that increasing the income of the richest class enables it to expand outward by buying more land. This reduces competition for more central land enabling the poorer classes to also expand outward and improve their utility levels. Conversely increasing the income of the poorer classes reduces the welfare of the rich, because it pushes the rich outward raising their transport costs. More recently, Pines and Sadka [136] generalized Wheaton's [176] comparative statics analysis to a fully closed city, with a single income group, in which aggregate land rent is redistributed equally among the residents. While they reestablish most of Wheaton's results, they show that the city's land area may decrease when population increases.

These analytical results ignore the fact that households of different income cannot possibly have identical preferences. As incomes increase preferences also change and it does not follow that the bid rent gradients for land become flatter functions of distance from the center with an increase in income. The question of the relationship between preferences, bid rents and various residential classes arose at the University of Pennyslvania in the late sixties where Britton Harris was attempting empirical applications of the Herbert and Stevens model [83], (see Section 3.3). This led to a Ph.D. dissertation by Wheaton [175] who examined the question empirically and later published some estimates of bid rent functions for the San Francisco area from a home interview sample collected in 1965 [180]. These results are subject to some statistical biases which are discussed in Anas [4; Ch. 1]. Nevertheless they were the first attempt to measure marginal rates of substitution among attributes such as the number of rooms, lot size, housing age and travel time. The empirical results showed some important differences in preferences (coefficients of utility functions) by income. The assumption of preferences invariant across income groups was no longer reasonable to maintain within urban economics, although it remains a mainstream implicit assertion in economic theory.

An insight which grew out of Wheaton's analysis is that the degree of the flattening of a bid rent curve by income depended crucially on two factors: "the preference for land or housing floor space" and "the value of commuting time." To see this consider that the household maximizes a utility function defined over Z, the composite commodity, Q, lot size, and t, time of travel to the center. Thus, we have the utility function $U(Z, Q, t)$ and the constraints $Y - Z - RQ - T(x) = 0$ and $H - t(x) - L(x) = 0$. Here, $T(x)$ and $t(x)$ are the exogeneously given travel cost and travel time functions of distance x, both of which increase with distance. Y is income and H is the total time budget to be divided between travel and leisure, L. Since $t(x)$ is exogenous and H fixed, $L(x)$ is determined as a residual. R is the bid rent of the household, which is an indifference curve between distance and rent. To see how this varies with distance we impose the conditions $dU = 0$ and $dY = 0$ and we obtain from these that

$$\frac{dR}{dx} = -\left[\frac{dT}{dx} - \left(\frac{\partial U/\partial t}{\partial U/\partial Z}\right)\frac{dt}{dx}\right]\Big/ Q.$$

The term in (.) is the "value of commuting time," or marginal rate of substitution between travel time and Z and is negative since

$\partial U/\partial t < 0$ by assumption. Since dT/dx and dt/dx are both positive it follows that $dR/dx < 0$. If rich (r) and poor (p) have the same utility function then,

$$\left(\frac{\partial U/\partial t}{\partial U/\partial Z}\right)\bigg|_p = \left(\frac{\partial U/\partial t}{\partial U/\partial Z}\right)\bigg|_r,$$

when the utility function is evaluated at the same Z, Q and t for both rich and poor. If $\bar{x}$ is the border between rich and poor, then it follows from the equation for dR/dx and the assumption that land is a normal good that $Q(\bar{x})_r > Q(\bar{x})_p$ and thus that the bid rent function for the rich at $\bar{x}$ is flatter than that for the poor at $\bar{x}$. If, however, we wish to take one step closer to realism we ought to recognize that the rich have higher values of time than do the poor, at the same Z, Q and t because they have different utility functions. This tends to make the bid rents of the rich steeper with distance favoring a more central location for them *unless* their preference for land increases sufficiently faster with income than their dislike for commuting (i.e. their value of time).

Wheaton [179] selected coefficients from his constant elasticity of substitution utility functions which he had estimated with the Bay Area data [180] and performed a simulation with five income groups in a monocentric setting parameterized to have a rough resemblance to the Bay Area. The value of time and the preference for land were the only two factors included in the utility functions, which were different by income group. The way such a simulation works is as follows: bid rent functions are computed for each income group given arbitrary levels of utility. One then orders the groups by the steepness of their bid rent functions in terms of their distance from the center and then computes to see if the ring which they can claim by being the highest bidders is wide enough to accommodate the quantity of land which they demand. One iterates this procedure by adjusting the levels of utility and recomputing the bid rent functions until the quantity of land demanded by each group is equal to the land allocated to that group at equilibrium in the ring reserved for that group. Thus, all households find a location at equilibrium. When one cannot preorder bid rent functions by steepness (because the elasticity of substitution varies between groups) the above procedure can be repeated by trial and error to find the order of each group at equilibrium.

Wheaton's simulation showed that despite differences in values of time and preferences for land caused by income, the five groups in equilibrium did order themselves according to increasing distance by income. This pattern, however, was not very stable: small perturbations within the estimated standard errors of the utility coefficients caused rich and poor households to flip locations in some cases. Wheaton conjectured that this instability was due to the fact that the preference for public goods, which increases by income, was not in the utility functions. Since the supply and quality of public goods increases with distance due to historical trends, the presence of public goods stabilizes a decentralized location for the rich.

Wheaton's conjecture remains a plausible but untested proposition. There has been relatively little interest in measuring the preference for public goods and services and no interest in pursuing further the question introduced by Wheaton. It may be observed that in many Latin American and other Third World cities, the rich often occupy central locations while the poor who have low values of time live in the "suburbs" (often squatter settlements) and commute by foot, bicycle or bus, inexpensive but time consuming means of transportation. It is also true, in many of these cities, that central locations have better public services and locational prestige than surrounding areas. It would appear that future work in monocentric simulation would do well to explain the location of different groups by income in an international context to see if different observed location patterns result from different parametrizations of the same theoretical model.

Analytical answers are difficult or nearly impossible to obtain when transport cost and travel time depend on income even if the utility function is constant with income. This issue arose in a paper by Wheaton [178] who conjectured incorrectly that the welfare results established by Hartwick, Schweizer and Varaiya [77] could be generalized to cases where transport cost depended on income. In such cases, Wheaton argued, the rich can have a steeper bid rent gradient, thus locating near the center. Increasing their income would increase their "value of time" making their bids even steeper and reducing competitive land market pressure on the surrounding poor, and thus raising the welfare of the poor. Similarly, increasing the income of the surrounding poor would steepen their bids putting pressure on the centrally located rich, and reducing their welfare. Arnott, MacKinnon and Wheaton [23] later investigated this problem and found two numerical counterexamples by means of monocentric simulation. These are based on the observation that the steepening of the bid rent gradient which occurs because transport costs depend on income, may be more than offset by an upward shift in the bid rent gradient which occurs because land is a normal good. This sort of analysis illustrates the use of simulation to check out a theoretical conjecture based on limited analytical models or faulty intuition. The insight derived from such "checks" is often impressive relative to the low cost of the simulation.

1.2. Congestion and the use of land for roads

The spatial effects of the urban traffic congestion externality forms a celebrated theme within theoretical urban economics. This is probably the most analyzed and overworked problem in both the theoretical and simulation literatures. It is also perhaps the only problem where numerical simulations have proved to be indispensable in firming up the theory. It is a theoretically important problem because it demonstrates the treatment of the theory of the second best in a spatial, urban context.

Traffic congestion arises because households living at different distances away from the center of the city arrive at work and leave for home at roughly the same time. Given a radial road network with certain road width, traffic would pile up into queues. However, in these stylized theoretical models the queueing aspect which stems from a traffic engineering perspective is neglected. Instead, travel cost and/or travel time on a short segment of a road during the rush hours is assumed to be an initially flat but later increasing (and strictly convex) function of the total traffic flowing through that road segment during the rush hour divided by the width (or capacity) of the road segment. This rather crude assumption is the same in the case of realistic network models in transportation planning. In that context, the assumption does much more violence than it does in the case of a monocentric city (see Section 3.1).

Analytically, the congestion phenomenon in a monocentric city is handled as follows. Let $n(x)$ be the number of households living at the thin annulus of width dx, x miles from the center. Then the number living beyond this radius is given by the integral,

$$N(x) = \int_x^{\bar{x}} n(s)\, ds$$

with $\bar{x}$ the edge of the city where the urban and agricultural land rents are equal. $N(x)$ is the volume of traffic (or flow) that must pass the circle at radius x, assuming that each household generates one vehicle trip. Then, the private (average) travel time (or travel cost) incurred by each vehicle in crossing the thin annulus of width dx at x is given by a function of the form,

$$t(x) = a_0 + a_1 \left[\frac{N(x)}{B(x)} \right]^{a_2},$$

where $t(x)$ is the per mile cost or time, a_0, a_1, a_2 are positive constants and $B(x)$ is the quantity of land in the thin annulus at x reserved for roads or the "road capacity" at x. Cost or time per mile is made a strictly convex increasing function of traffic volume $N(x)$ by choosing $a_2 > 1$. The above function is almost universally employed and corresponds to the Bureau of Public Roads function employed in practical network equilibrium models. In that function, $a_1 = 0.15$ and $a_2 = 4.0$. An exception to the above function is the alternative,

$$t(x) = a_0 \exp\left\{ a_1 \left[\frac{N(x)}{B(x)} \right]^{a_2} \right\}$$

where a_0, $a_1 > 0$ and $a_2 \geq 1$. This was introduced by Arnott and MacKinnon [22]. They employed this function because the elasticity of private congestion with respect to flow exceeds unity and because the ratio of the marginal congestion externality to private congestion is an increasing function of flow. Arnott and MacKinnon refer to these two properties as stylized facts proposed by Solow [156] and Vickrey [171] respectively.

The traffic congestion problem in long run monocentric analysis takes several forms. One is to take as given a reasonable allocation of land to roads described by the function $B(x)$. Given this predetermined $B(x)$ one then solves for the usual land use equilibrium rent and population density gradients and also for the transport expenditure gradient $t(x)$ under the assumption that vehicles incur their private average expenditure at every distance x. This is a second best analysis in two respects: because it takes $B(x)$ as predetermined, and essentially arbitrary, and because it assumes that there is no congestion toll to extract from each vehicle the marginal expenditure it imposes on itself and on other vehicles. It is known from first best analysis that each vehicle should incur not its average cost $t(x)$ but $t(x) + N(x)[\partial t(x)/\partial N(x)]$, its full marginal expenditure. In a city of households with identical preferences this marginal cost pricing strategy maximizes the common long run equilibrium utility level, given a road width function $B(x)$. The second form of the problem is to determine, within the analysis, the function $B(x)$, i.e. an allocation of land to roads in the first best or second best sense. Again, the first best function $B(x)$ is the one which, together with the simultaneously determined congestion toll maximizes the common utility level. As we shall see, a number of second best formulations are possible and these center on how to determine $B(x)$ given that levying a marginal cost congestion toll is not possible.

Before we discuss the use of simulation to solve the above problems we ought to briefly review the early analytical results. These are due primarily to Strotz [159], Mills and DeFerranti [128], Solow and Vickrey [157] and Livesey [112]. Strotz in 1965, stated and examined the first best tolling and allocation problem for a city with discrete rings. Mills and DeFerranti in 1971 posed the first best problem as the minimization of total development cost within the residential part of a monocentric city, assuming households everywhere in the city consumed the same and fixed lot size. The road width function, $B(x)$, being a policy instrument, the analysis becomes a calculus of variations problem. Solow and Vickrey in 1972 examined the first best problem in a thin rectangular business district and Livesey in 1973 reformulated the Mills and DeFerranti problem taking into account transport congestion within as well as outside of the central business district (CBD) and making the CBD radius endogenous. For our purposes the chief analytical finding, not invalidated by numerous extensions of these early models, is this: if the CBD radius is given (say x) then the first best allocation of land to roads, $B(x)$, is a concave decreasing function reaching zero at the urban fringe when population size is small (curve 1 in Figure 1(a)). For larger population sizes road width is again concave

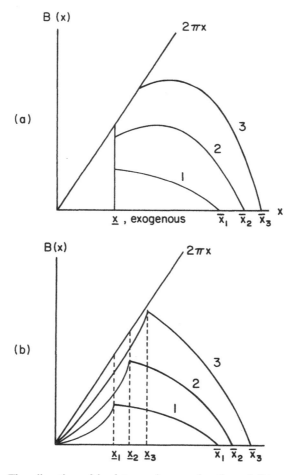

FIGURE 1 The allocation of land to roads, as a function of distance from the center in a circular city.

but increases as we move away from the CBD fringe decreasing thereafter (curve 2 in Figure 1(a)) and when population size is sufficiently larger all of the land in a band around the CBD may go to roads, but eventually road width, which is still concave, again peaks and declines thereafter reaching zero at the fringe (curve 3 in Figure 1(a)). Livesey's contribution [112] was to show that the above awkward result was due to the fact that the CBD radius was exogenous and intra-CBD transport not explicitly modeled. He showed that if this shortcoming is remedied then road width is convex and increasing with distance within the CBD and concave and decreasing with distance in the surburban ring with the peak always occurring at the CBD boundary and never taking up all the land at this boundary (see Figure 1(b)). Another analytically established result is that it is optimal to tolerate some congestion level around the CBD. An earlier speculation by Beckmann [28] that congestion should be uniform everywhere is thus shown to be incorrect. Also, with congestion tolls the city is more compact (smaller radius) and has higher land use density.

Given these analytical results, why is there a need to apply numerical simulation? There are several reasons. First, because transport expenditure and/or road width are endogenously determined, a qualitative comparative static analysis is very difficult and has not been attempted. Second, because first best congestion tolls are in general impractical to levy and because transport planners allocate land to roads inefficiently, there is a need to examine the effects of various distortions and to compare first best and second best as well as various second best allocations to each other. Of particular interest is the question of how a transport planner should conduct cost-benefit analysis in a second best world.

Perhaps the most complete simulation model incorporating traffic congestion was published by Dixit [46]. The chief contribution of this paper was the investigation of an optimum population size for a fully closed city given that production in the CBD is characterized by increasing returns to scale with land and labor hours as inputs. The size of the CBD is endogenous but travel within it is ignored, households have a Cobb–Douglas utility function defined over the composite commodity and land, subject to a time budget constraint with each household supplying a fixed number of hours for the sum of work and commuting. Dixit assumed $a_2 = 1$ in the congestion function. Unlike Mills and DeFerranti [128], he allowed households to choose lot size and consumption according to their location. He also assumed that all of the composite commodity produced in the CBD is locally consumed and that all rents are redistributed equally among residents. Under the assumption that wages are equal to marginal products, increasing returns to scale would mean that the city ought to be of an infinite size were it not for the cost of commuting. Even without traffic congestion, a city of large enough radius would cause the households' equal equilibrium utility level to eventually peak at a finite population size, as increases in transport expenditure for fringe residents outweigh increases in wages from the addition of residents. To the extent that traffic congestion increases transport expenditure, it helps achieve a smaller optimum population size. What Dixit was able to show is that given his plausible parameter values, optimal population size was reached at about 200,000 households or 600,000 to 750,000 people. He concludes that "... the model cannot explain Chicago as an optimum town. This is probably equally the fault of the model and of Chicago." He also found, however, that the results were very sensitive to the value of a_1 so that halving it doubled the optimal population size showing the importance of transport congestion technology on optimal size. He showed that wages as a function of size peak after utility. Wages peak because in large cities less time is available for work and more is spent in commuting. Dixit concluded that if wages (instead of utilities) are used to determine optimal size, then a substantial error may occur. He showed also that no more than 75% of the land at the edge of the CBD was allocated to roads. Dixit's most surprising result, which invalidates Wheaton's [176] comparative static analysis for an uncongested city, was that both CBD and city radii were not monotonically increasing functions of population but rather that both peaked but after optimal population size was achieved. He explained this as follows: "... commuting in these very congested towns takes a large amount of time, leaving little time for work and leading to low levels of output. The marginal utility of output then rises, and it is no longer worthwhile to pay rent for the larger area of land" ([46]; p. 648). It was mentioned in the introduction that Pines and Sadka [136] have more recently confirmed this result in a theoretical monocentric analysis with rent redistribution but without a production sector.

The major shortcoming of Dixit's otherwise very detailed model was the neglect of congestion within the CBD. A model which properly treats this and expands on Livesey's [112] analytical result is by Sullivan [162, 163]. In this model residents choose a home in the suburbs and a workplace in the CBD. The first-best optimum city (one with congestion tolls and optimum road width) has a more

dispersed distribution of employment (larger CBD) but more
concentrated distribution of residences than in an equilibrium
model in which tolls are not levied but road width is still optimally
selected. Roads in the equilibrium city are too wide both within and
outside of the CBD. The part of these results which pertains to the
suburban ring were already known from earlier analyses and
simulations such as those of Mills [125], Muth [133], Solow [156],
Henderson [81] and Arnott and MacKinnon [22]. However, while
Arnott and MacKinnon computed efficiency gains (from tolls) of
0.068% of income, Sullivan [163] finds much larger gains of 1.91%
of income or 8.25% of transportation cost. It is not possible to tell
with certainty to what degree such large differences are due to
differences in parameters. Sullivan [163] argues convincingly that
the larger gains are due to the inclusion of the CBD land use, since
congestion in the CBD is the most severe due to high land prices
and thus narrow streets. In the open city, a congestion toll policy
causes the city to increase in population. The same result is
obtained by Henderson [81] who simulates an open city neglecting
land use and transport within the CBD. First best analysis of
congested cities are only of limited value. The reasons are two.
First, congestion tolls are generally difficult, if not impossible, to
levy and too costly to administer. Sullivan [163] puts this as follows:
"in our computed cities, toll booths would be placed at 0.06-mile
intervals, meaning that the average commuter would stop 104 times
every day to pay tolls." Thus, there is interest in examining second
best situations in which tolls are not levied, or a uniform toll (or
gasoline tax) is used instead as a second-best policy instrument.
There are other alternatives such as transit fare subsidies. These
may be viewed as second best means of reducing auto traffic
congestion. Second, even in a second best treatment of congestion
pricing, it is difficult, if not impossible, to derive the second best
optimal road width without knowing the utility function(s) of city
residents. In practice transportation planners can at best hope to
determine such an allocation by using stylized rules of thumb from
applied cost-benefit analysis. Thus, there is an interest in examining
how such rules of thumb would distort highway planning decisions.

One may explore these issues in a variety of ways. For example,
one may examine the distortive effects of various second best
congestion pricing strategies given a reasonable predetermined or

second best optimal road width decision. Alternatively, one can examine different road planning schemes given a second best congestion pricing scheme. Sullivan [163] and Henderson [81] have examined numerically the effects of a gasoline tax. The former author does so for his model which includes CBD land use, while the latter does so for the residential ring of an open city. Sullivan reports that the per capita welfare gain is 30% of the welfare gain from the first best congestion toll policy.

The problem of second best road widths has received substantial attention. The first extensive numerical investigation of this issue was done by Mills [125]. This, incidentally, was the first and probably best documented numerical simulation of a monocentric city, setting the style for later work. It is apparent from this work that Mills labored carefully over the selection of parameters and the application of sensitivity analysis to each parameter in order to perform a full comparative static perturbation of his model. Mills developed two versions of the model. One in which there are no congestion tolls and drivers incur only average private costs of travel. In this model Mills assumed $a_2 = 2$ i.e. a nonlinear and strictly convex congestion function and that $B(x) = B$, a constant allocation of land to roads. Even though a year earlier the Mills and DeFerranti [128] paper had established the optimality of a decreasing or inverted U-shaped land allocation, empirical scrutiny suggested a more uniform or somewhat increasing road width with distance from the center. Mills's chosen value of B was such as to give roughly 20% of an urban area's land to roads. While a constant B may represent an arbitrary planning decision, Mills also examined what would occur if the transport sector bought land and priced travel as if it were a competitive industry. Under this scenario, the price of transportation services at each distance x is equal to the land rent needed to bid away the road at that location and enough land is allocated to roads to equate demanded and supplied transport services. Mills' simulations showed that this pricing scheme put more land into roads near the center and less at the periphery thus greatly reducing congestion near the center and enabling residents to live further away, producing a larger and lower density urban area.

Solow [156] developed a model of the residential ring assuming $a_2 = 1$ and analyzed it numerically. Solow assumed that the fraction of land devoted to roads is a decreasing linear function of distance from the center say $1 - bx$. Then, the quantity of land devoted to roads is the quadratic $B(x) = 2\pi x - 2\pi b x^2$. This function resembles the first best allocation function which we already discussed. Given a specific value of b Solow was able to solve for equilibrium in the residential ring without tolls, and by repetition he was able to find the optimal value of b. Solow then attempted to simulate the behavior of a road planner. Such a planner would be tempted to evaluate the benefits of a road-widening in travel expenditures saved and the costs incurred as the additional land that must be purchased. By means of numerical examples, Solow showed that the distorted rent gradient which does not include the effects of first best toll pricing is such that the road planner would move away from the maximum utility road width in the direction of building too many roads. This conclusion was based on Solow's impression that the market land rent gradient of his model was *everywhere* below the shadow land rent gradient that would occur if congestion tolls were levied.

Arnott and MacKinnon [22], in a paper which generated a rich variety of results, showed by means of a simulation model that Solow's argument which represented conventional wisdom was faulty. Their analysis is based on the following calculation of *two* shadow rents at a particular location in a city with an arbitrary (second best) road width function. The first is the shadow rent on land in residential use. It is computed by adding a small amount of residential land at a location and solving for a new equilibrium after using lump sum government transfers to insure that utility levels remain fixed at their previous levels. The shadow rent on residential land is then the money saved by the government divided by the amount of land that was added. The second shadow rent is computed in the same way but the small amount of land is used to widen the road at that location. This compensated approach differs from Solow's evaluation of benefits who, as we saw above, assumed that the social value of a road-widening was equal to the direct transport savings created by the land addition. Arnott and MacKinnon's approach corrects this by taking into account the long run lot size adjustments which occur when roads are widened or when residential land is increased. The authors thus derive *three* rent gradients numerically; the shadow rent on land in residences, the shadow rent on land in roads and the market rent on land in residences. They demonstrate by simulation that when lot sizes are fixed then the shadow rent on residential land exceeds the market rent. When lot sizes are not fixed this generally occurs near the center of the city with the market rent exceeding the shadow rent further away from the center. The shadow rent on land in transportation need not be anchored at the agricultural rent at the urban fringe. In one simulation the authors used a greatly suboptimal road width function. This road narrowed to about six miles from the center then suddenly widening and remaining so. The shadow rent on land in roads decreased with distance from the center becoming negative just before the road widened.

A conclusion of the Arnott and MacKinnon paper is that since the correct shadow rent on residential land does not everywhere exceed the market rent, planners may allocate land to roads until the shadow rent on land in roads equals the market rent and not end up putting too much land in roads as Solow and others had concluded. Unfortunately, Arnott and MacKinnon do not examine to see whether the conventional wisdom is really reversed in an *empirically* realistic simulation. Perhaps the most important conclusion of their paper is that the cost-benefit calculations of any road planner must utilize a complex and realistic urban simulation model: no simple yet reliable rules of thumb have been found.

1.3. Other themes in general equilibrium simulation

It is important to point out that "general equilibrium simulation" or "applied general equilibrium analysis" is a relatively new area within economics. In this context, there is an aspatial literature which has emerged roughly at the same time and independently of the monocentric literature. Illustrative articles from this literature can be found in an edited book by Scarf and Shoven [147]. The literature is due primarily to a series of papers by Shoven and Whalley [152, 153, 154] where the theory of general equilibrium and fixed point computational techniques have been invoked to investigate the effects of various taxation schemes. Two of the articles in this aspatial literature come close to urban economics because they are concerned with housing.

The article by Devarajan, Fullerton and Musgrave [44] examines the effects of taxes on various goods and the distribution of their burdens among different income classes. Housing is selected as a good with very high capital to labor ratio and a necessity—housing expenditures as a proportion of income decline with income of the consumer. Income tax rebates (due to the deductibility of the property tax) are also taken into account. It is shown that the cum-tax price changes are regressive but the income effect is progressive, and the two combine to a net regressive change in real after tax income.

Hamilton and Whalley [70] extend a paper by Fullerton, Shoven and Whalley [64] which uses dynamic (sequenced) general equi-librium simulations to examine the effects of replacing the U.S. income tax with a progressive consumption tax. Hamilton and Whalley's paper introduces a second asset: housing. They also use Canadian parameters. They focus on the treatment of housing under the income tax. Their model can sort out the relative sizes of the interasset and intertemporal distortion effects associated with alternative housing taxation schemes. They find that taxing imputed housing income improves welfare because the removal of the inter-asset distortion effect of the present Canadian tax treatment outweighs the gain from improved intertemporal consumption allocation.

While the above articles have not directly influenced the mono-centric literature, they do raise questions that may be readdressed within a spatial context, in the future.

There are a number of themes in monocentric general equi-librium simulation investigated by Arnott and MacKinnon. These are the effects of urban transportation changes with particular attention paid on the location of various income groups [20], the incidence in the long run of changes in the residential property tax [21] and the effects of building height restrictions [19]. There are also four papers by Sullivan. In two of these [165, 164] he studies the incidence and excess burdens of the residential and industrial property taxes respectively. The other two [161, 166] deal with the spatial effects of scale and agglomeration economies in production. Taxes are also examined by Hobson [85].

In the first article [20], Arnott and MacKinnon investigated how changes in the cost structure of different travel modes would influence switching among modes, changes in overall welfare and its distribution and changes in urban land area and building densities.

Their model included two income groups with different incomes and tastes, each group deriving utility from housing (produced using land and structures), other goods and leisure. Both the money and time costs of transportation entered the household's calculus. This model would not differ much from Wheaton's simulation [179] discussed earlier (see Section 1.1) were it not for the realistic inclusion of four travel modes available to both groups. These are walking, bus (or public transportation), inexpensive car and expensive car. The authors treat these modes carefully, distinguishing them by cost and time and with adequate attention paid to fixed costs such as parking and distance related costs such as gasoline expense but ignoring congestion. The authors compute ordinary equilibria in which the incomes of each group are prespecified and remain fixed, equilibrium levels of utility being determined by the model. They also compute compensated equilibria in which incomes are allowed to vary so that each group attains a prespecified utility level same as that in the base case. If post-compensation net government revenues are positive the change being simulated has positive aggregate benefits since it is possible to make one group better off without making another worse off. In the authors' base simulation the land use pattern corresponds to the stylized standard case with all the poor living near the center walking or taking the bus to work, with the rich being located more peripherally and driving. Attention is focused on whether changes in the cost and time characteristics of modes can greatly disturb the long run location of the two groups. For example, a large parking tax induces some of the rich who drive, to relocate near the center outbidding the poor there and switching to walking and bus in order to avoid the high parking costs. This results in three groups of rings occupied by rich, poor and rich respectively. More complex ring patterns are also easily generated. The authors document the interesting fact that transportation savings provide an underestimate of aggregate benefits from a transportation improvement but not by more than 10%. This is done by comparing transportation savings with a measure of benefit computed by applying the computed marginal utility of income to the change in utility due to the transportation policy. They also report that in all cases the absolute value of the change in differential land rents is always smaller than the absolute value of aggregated uncompensated benefits to renters.

In the second article [21], Arnott and MacKinnon examined the

incidence and excess burden of a uniform equal-rate *ad valorem* tax
on residential structures and land. The paper is a counterpoint to
the conventional view which argues incorrectly that the supply of
structures is perfectly elastic and the supply of land perfectly
inelastic, therefore the portion of the property tax which falls on
structures is borne by the renter while the portion falling on land is
borne by the landowner. In the long run a property tax change can
induce the city's area to change thus the supply of land is not
perfectly inelastic. Also, Grieson [68] pointed out that an increase
in the quantity of structures in the long run causes the average
height of buildings in a city to increase. With a building technology
in which the marginal cost of a story increases with the number of
stories, an increase in the quantity of structures causes the average
price of structures to rise. The authors contrast this view with
Muth's [132] conventional view who assumes a perfectly elastic
supply of structures but allows for land, in addition to structures, to
enter the utility function. The authors simulate cities in which
households have identical preferences and incomes. Thus the
question of incidence focuses on the distribution of the loss between
the landlords or government (this loss is equal to the change in
differential land rents) and the residents. The loss to residents is
computed as either a general equilibrium compensating variation
loss ("the amount of income that given to city residents in the
posttax situation would make them just as well off as they were in
the pretax situation") or as a general equilibrium equivalent
variation loss ("the amount of income that, taken away from city
residents in the pretax situation, would make them just as well off
as they are in the posttax situation"). The authors show that
landlords bear 12.7% and 13.4% of the burden of the tax, smaller
than the land share in housing rents (14.3% and 14.8% with and
without the tax). Residents (i.e. tenants) bear the full burden of the
structures component of the tax and part of the burden of the land
component of the tax since the supply of land in residential land use
is not completely inelastic.

A 25% property tax results in a 22.8% increase in the average
price of housing gross of tax. The authors also calculate the excess
burden of the tax as the difference between tax revenues less the
decrease in aggregate differential land rents. Then they compute
compensating and equivalent variations in (post- and pretax)

incomes. Compensating and equivalent variation excess burdens are 8.5% and 8.1% of net property tax revenues respectively. However marginal excess burdens are 18.3% when one goes from a 24% to a 26% property tax city. An even more interesting result is that a 20% housing subsidy completely neutralizes the effects of the 25% property tax. The average price of housing net of tax increases by only 1.6%. Grieson and Muth cities are found to be very similar suggesting that the effects of the property tax may be insensitive to assumptions about building technology.

The two papers by Sullivan [164, 165] which also deal with the incidence of the property tax, are fashioned after his spatial monocentric model reviewed in Section 1.2. In this model residents choose a home in the suburbs and a workplace in the CBD and thus both CBD and suburban ring land uses are endogenous. Therefore, both industrial and residential property taxes can be investigated and their effects on general equilibrium land use can be traced for both parts of the city. Finally, his models include a labor market which is manifested in the endogenized CBD. In [165], Sullivan considers the replacement of a nondistortionary land tax in a small open city with the residential property tax. This reduces the density, population and land area of the open city. If such a city is embedded into a closed region, production and jobs shift to other cities within the region, the net return on land increasing in other cities within the region at the expense of the city implementing the tax change. In aggregate, landowners benefit while residents lose. The excess burden of the property tax is 6.5% of total tax revenue. In [164] we see a similar analysis carried out with the same model, with the exception that the nondistortionary land tax is replaced by a tax on industrial property in the CBD. The numerical simulations in the two papers are very comparable and so are the results, the excess burden of the industrial property tax being 4.5% of property tax revenue.

Recently Hobson [85] has written a paper in which there is endogenous CBD and suburban residential land use but intra-CBD commuting is ignored. The model city is open to migration and wages are endogenous. He uses this model to compare the tax burden and dead weight losses of: a residential property tax, a wage tax, an output tax and a sales tax. His results imply that output, sales and wage taxes are less distortionary than the property taxes but place bigger burdens on residents. In jurisdictions where residents benefit from public goods, these taxes may be preferable to property taxes.

In their third article [19], Arnott and MacKinnon measure the costs of height restrictions in a long run general equilibrium analysis of a monocentric city without CBD land use. Their simulation treats discrete housing technologies corresponding to buildings of different heights and utilizes actual construction cost data to create cost functions. Households derive utility from floor space, not caring about the story in which they live. They also derive utility from the open recreational land associated with structures of different heights, and from travel time. The authors show that with their realistic cost functions, if the assumption is made that no utility is derived from open space, then simulated cities of about one million in population turn out to be too small and too dense. Allowing open space to be important results in realistic land use patterns. For example, ". . . buildings near the center are nineteen stories tall, and building heights decline gradually to a distance of about six miles from the center, where they drop sharply from eight to two stories," which cover the last 71% of the city's residential area. Next, the authors consider introducing ten and five story height restrictions over the entire area of a city such as the one described above. The authors show that height restrictions reduce land rents near the center (where they are binding) but greatly increase them elsewhere as the demand spills outward in the long run. Aggregate land rents are increased and landlords gain. If households care strongly about recreational open space they sub- stitute this for structures when height restrictions are introduced. This reduces the cost of height restrictions. The authors calculate that the ten story restriction costs each household (of income $14,000) just $22 a year. This implies that height restrictions may well be worth imposing if they have substantial external benefits.

The last two papers by Sullivan [161, 166] focus on external scale economies in production and agglomerative economies in office employment. In [161], firms in the CBD produce an export good using capital, labor and land as inputs under internal constant returns to scale, thus treating input and output prices as fixed. However, the production technology summarized in the unit cost function has an external scale economy component which reduces average cost as aggregate export output rises. Both CBD and residential ring land uses are endogenous as in all of Sullivan's models and the allocation of land to roads is determined by a production function which combines capital and land. The transport planner determines transport service capacity at each point in the city by equating marginal resource costs with marginal benefits measured by reduced commuting time. The city is closed in the sense that all land rent is redistributed to residents, but open in the sense that labor migration is allowed. Meeting labor demand allows endogenous determination of wages at each point in the CBD. Aggregate labor demand determines population size. Housing in the residential ring is produced by land and capital inputs at constant returns. This model is the most detailed and realistic monocentric general equilibrium model and can be applied to a wide range of policy questions. Some variants of this model were applied to second best road planning as we saw in Section 1.2 and to the incidence of the property tax as we saw in this section. It appears, however, that questions centered around the external scale economy have not yet been explored adequately.

In [166], Sullivan extends the above model to analyze an urban form resembling a modern, rather than 19th century, monocentric city. The CBD is occupied by offices subject to an agglomerative economy of face to face contacts while manufacturing occurs all along a decentralized ring around a circumferential highway at an exogenous distance from the office-CBD. This suburban manufacturing ring is called the SBD (for "suburban business district"). Both CBD and SBD land uses are endogenous, CBD workers locate in the rings around the CBD and SBD workers locate on both sides of the SBD. Land values peak at the CBD center and peak locally around the circumferential highway.

Sullivan uses this model to examine the effects of CBD and suburban residential density restrictions on urban form. The results are clarifying of intuitively expected changes. CBD density restrictions are given the form of a maximum capital to land ratio. Because of external scale economies capital to land ratios throughout the CBD are decreased. CBD land rents decrease and SBD land rents increase. CBD radius is decreased. Total employment decreases (the city is open to migration) with a smaller decrease in the SBD. Wages decrease with larger decreases in the CBD wage.

Housing density controls increase wages and the share of employment in the CBD. Land rents in the unzoned area also increase.

1.4. Computational techniques

All of the simulations discussed above share the common characteristic that they are long run general equilibrium simulations of a
monocentric city. As such they require essentially the same computational tasks. These may be summarized as follows.

1) Identify each distinct land user group (of firms or households)
that can possibly appear in the long run equilibrium solution.

2) Given the number of actors (households, firms) in each group
allocate them into a ring (or rings) around the center and to given
discrete situations such as buildings or travel modes in such a way
that the following equilibrium conditions are satisfied:

i) each land user group is the highest bidder for land in the
ring(s) in which it is located and the market rent for land in that
ring equals this highest bid,

ii) given the market rents of all the locations, each land user
group maximizes its objective (utility or profit) in the ring(s) to
which it is allocated, competitive firms making zero profit,

iii) all members of each user group are located somewhere,

iv) at the boundary between adjacent rings allocated to two land
user groups, the two groups are equal bidders and at the boundary
of the city, the user group in the last ring bids the agricultural (and
exogenous) land rent.

These requirements apply to a closed city for which group sizes
are given. In an open city, utility or profit levels for each user group
are given and group sizes are determined within the model,
assuming free migration into and out of the city.

A number of alternative approaches have been taken in implementing the above procedure computationally. To this author's
knowledge Dixit [46] is the only contributor who was bold enough
to treat space (distance) as a continuous variable in a complex
numerical model. He then characterizes the equilibrium conditions

described above by means of a system involving differential equations defined over distance with appropriate boundary conditions. He obtains the solution using a computer package which directly solves this system of differential equations. This is probably the most ambitious computational approach used in the literature. It is well suited to Dixit's problem who has to solve a differential equation to find the first-best road width function.

Other authors treat distance as a discrete variable dividing the land around the center into "thin" annuli of equal widths. Sullivan [163], for example, uses a width of 0.06 miles, Arnott and MacKinnon [22] use 0.25 miles, and Mills [125] 0.1 miles. Land use and prices within an annulus are assumed to be homogeneous or to occur at the midpoint of the annulus. The use of such discrete representations provides a very close approximation to reality and offers the great advantage of having to deal with correspondences rather than functions. Thus, it is easy to introduce policy instruments and exogeneous changes which vary discontinuously with distance.

It is clear from the literature that within such a discrete representation, there are essentially two types of computational approaches for obtaining solutions. One of these I will call the *Iterative Bid Rent Methods* (IBRM), the other I will call the *Fixed Point Methods* (FPM). The IBRM were implemented almost universally in the earlier simulations prior to the work of MacKinnon [116, 117] who introduced the FPM. The IBRM work as follows for a closed city.

One begins with arbitrary utility or profit levels for each group of land users, and computes demanded or supplied consumption and production decisions at each distance given these utility and profit levels. Given these decisions, the bid rent of each use for each ring is computed and each group is allocated to those rings where it is the highest bidder. One then computes the excess demand (or supply) of land to each land user group by seeing if the land area of the rings allocated to it exceeded or fall short of its aggregate demanded land quantity. If there is excess demand, utility and profit levels are lowered and if there is excess supply they are raised and the next iteration is performed. Iterations continue until excess demands or some other convergence criteria are arbitrarily close to zero. It is easy to show that if a solution is found it does satisfy the conditions of equilibrium. To my knowledge no proofs of convergence have been presented but the approach seems to work well in all reported applications. It is important to note that the IBRM can also be applied with continuous bid-rent functions provided that one can search and find at each iteration, the points where these functions intersect with each other. Doing so, however, does not seem to offer a great advantage and to my knowledge has been applied only by Solow [156] who appears a bit disappointed with the quality of his numerical results even though he deals with only one land user group but in a model that includes congestion. One often has to perform outer iterations in order to compute correctly various adjustments such as income from land, lump sum transfers to achieve compensation or external effects such as congested traffic flow. The pioneering numerical study by Mills [125] which included congestion, the paper by Wheaton [179] which examined location by income, are examples of the bid rent method. While it has never been used in simulation, a more efficient computational procedure is provided in Fujita [60] for the simple case where bid-rent curves can be pre-ordered by steepness.

Later work and in particular the simulations by Arnott and MacKinnon [19, 20, 21, 22] and Sullivan [161, 162, 163, 164, 165, 166] use the fixed point methods developed for the computation of general economic equilibria. These methods are also known as "simplicial search algorithms" or as "Scarf's algorithm" [146]. The adaptation of these methods to the case of spatial monocentric models is due to MacKinnon [116, 117], King [100, 101] and Richter [141, 142, 143].

The basic idea of the fixed point approach is that any general equilibrium system is completely solvable once the equilibrium prices are found. Then, all physical allocations can be determined by means of side computations. Since there are as many unknown prices as "commodities" in the market less one arbitrary price, it is possible to normalize the unknown prices so that they sum to unity. (This defines a special type of set called a simplex). Next, since the demand functions (or correspondances) are homogeneous of degree zero one can write the excess demand function for each commodity i as $G_i(\bar{P})$, where $\bar{P}$ is the normalized price vector. At equilibrium, $G_i(\bar{P}) \leq 0$ and $G_i(\bar{P})P_i = 0$ for all i. The above framework is common to all the algorithms which differ only in the methods of price adjustment and search strategy in the simplicial space. MacKinnon [117] has discussed some of the mathematical tricks that come in handy in constructing a particular algorithm and has reported on the performance of the "Vector Sandwich Method" (Kuhn and MacKinnon [106]), to a variety of problems in spatial economics and in particular to monocentric models.

The difficulty in the application of fixed point methods in spatial economics stems from the fact that land in each location must be treated as a separate commodity. At equilibrium, land in many locations is consumed by only one group. Whereas in the aspatial economic models each commodity is usually consumed by each group. More importantly in the aspatial economy demand depends on prices, income and preferences whereas in the spatial economy it also depends on locational choice. Thus the difference between spatial and nonspatial application hinges on the computation of demands. King [100] has proposed a version of Scarf-type algorithms which circumvents this difficulty. Normally a spatial economy would consist of m zones, n commodities and k consumers. He proposed increasing the number of commodities to $n + k$ adding k "artificial commodities" with spatially invariant prices. He also assumed that each of these artificial commodities can be produced in each of the m zones, thus augmenting the number of production functions by $k \times m$. In the transformed model, production of the ith artificial commodity in zone j is equivalent to the location of the ith type of household or firm in j and the quantity produced of the ith commodity is the level of utility or profit. King is able to show that such a solution is more efficient than MacKinnon's approach which must keep track of household locations in computing demands at each iteration. King also shows that the algorithm's converged solution satisfies the equilibrium conditions. He applied the procedure to test its performance and reports, among other results, that computation time rises roughly with n^4 where n is the number of commodities.

The above computational approaches are suited to a general equilibrium spatial economy in which production is competitive (no economies of scale), there are no externalities and no public sectors, namely no tax rates and municipal budgets. Problems in which the above occur all have common characteristics which require that the above computational techniques be applied iteratively. This has been the subject of some investigation by MacKinnon [117] and King [101] who apply their respective algorithms iteratively. The key difference is that the above complications introduce additional equations that must hold at equilibrium but usually there are no new "prices" that will balance these equations. An exception to this is the public sector where a tax rate acts as a "price" to balance the municipal budget, but this equation does not necessarily resemble an excess demand function. King [101] has written clearly on this subject. He formulates the utility and profit maximization problems of households and firms conditional on the anticipated level of each externality. Furthermore, these anticipations must be formulated consistently so that when all excess demands vanish at equilibrium, anticipated and actual externality levels are equal. A standard application is that of traffic congestion discussed in Section 1.2. Here, the externality is travel time and if one sets the problem up correctly, at equilibrium anticipated and actual travel times will be identical.

Externalities and scale economies can create multiple equilibria as is well known. It is very difficult in general to identify the presence of more than one equilibrium position. I know of no simulation in the monocentric literature which points out such a result. The urban externality problem *par excellence* is, as we saw, the traffic congestion problem and in this context the uniqueness and stability of equilibrium has not been the object of attention but rather an assumed property in the absence of any computational evidence to the contrary.

1.5. Dynamics

An area of recent interest within urban economics is the controversial development of dynamic models of urban land use. These are discussed in other volumes, but here I wish to focus on the uses of simulation to test some very different ideas within this young literature.

An interesting result which arises in dynamic models in which developers have foresight into the future, is the timing of development. Often, future development of a lot can yield a higher present value of profits than current development of it. Then, it will be Pareto efficient to postpone development till the optimal date. In fact this insight was first demonstrated by means of numerical examples by Pines [135] and Ohls and Pines [134]. Their argument may be explained as follows. Consider a two ring monocentric city and assume that population growth occurs in two discrete periods. There will be a trade-off between redevelopment costs and travel costs. If the former are sufficiently high relative to the latter, it will be efficient to substitute extra travel for redevelopment and develop the second ring first at the lower densities it would require, filling in the inner ring during the second period. This avoids (or greatly minimizes) redevelopment costs at the expense of more commuting (to the center) during the first period. If redevelopment costs are very low relative to travel costs, then it will be efficient to develop the first ring in period one and redevelop it and also build the second ring in period two, thus saving travel cost in the first period. Apparently unaware of these contributions, Wheaton [181] has recently simulated a monocentric city demonstrating that it is, in some cases, efficient to develop it from the outside toward the inside. What is significant in Wheaton's analysis, but not stressed by him, is that the leap-frogging over land can be efficient even in the absence of redevelopment costs. In the same simulation he also finds that residential density can increase with distance from the center, a result which was derived theoretically in a model by Anas [3] under the assumption that developers are myopic.

In another paper, Wheaton [182] uses a monocentric model of myopic development behavior adapted from Anas [3] to see if redevelopment of the central housing area of a city takes place before abandonment of it. Anas [3] had shown that when income increases rapidly over time the quasi-bid-rent on centrally located structures built in the past can fall and become negative causing households to abandon these obsolete structures for new ones in the fringes of the city. Clearly this result depends on the assumption of sufficiently high redevelopment costs. Wheaton's simulations show that central areas will be redeveloped before they are abandoned, but he ignores demolition and other adjustment costs in doing so. Empirically, the proposition advanced by Anas [3] seems to hold. McDonald and Bowman [120] later published a paper showing that land values in the Chicago area had a humped shape with a local minimum just outisde of the central business district (CBD). Abandonment is not uncommon in these areas.

A major piece of work in dynamic monocentric simulation based on partially actual data has been undertaken by Fujita and Kashiwadani [61, 62]. In this work the degree of attention paid to actual data is modest. Yet their model is still greatly oversimplified and treats the Tokyo region as a monocentric area. The authors divide the Tokyo region into 21 "concentric" zonal areas and define three households types, manufacturing firms and local service firms as the only land uses. As in Fujita's theoretical model [59], they assume a one to one correspondence between activity types and building types. They neglect deterioration and demolition. They treat locational interactions among land use activities by defining activity complexes. Each such complex consists of a set of activities which always locate together in fixed proportions. It includes, for example, some local employment together with households. The authors perform two simulations of Tokyo for the time period 1955–2000. One of these solve for the efficient spatial development pattern *ex post facto*, by fixing the total demand for buildings of each type in each year from 1955 to 1975 to the actual demand value for that year. The second simulation is similar except that it includes the institutional practice in Tokyo where CBD employers pay their employees' travel costs, more than half of the employees in the region being in this category. Projections are used for the total demand by building type during the periods beyond 1975. The Tokyo model generates sprawl as activity complexes are developed outward from the center. Comparing these results to the actual growth path in the period 1955–1975 the authors find that the actual path has more sprawl than the *ex post facto* optimal one and that it has much higher land prices in the suburban areas. These results apparently recur under various projections of total demands for the periods 1975–2000. One is tempted—as the authors do—to argue that market agents are overspeculating. How does the market sustain much higher than optimal land prices over such a long time period? It appears to me that this result may be largely due to the model's oversimplifying assumptions: some missing variables, household classification and the lack of realistic utility functions. Were this not so, the result contradicts the hypothesis of rationally adaptive expectations in land markets.

1.6. Non-monocentric models

An obvious question which arises from a survey of the monocentric literature is whether there will be an equally prosperous and exciting literature on polycentric or nomonocentric urban configurations. And if so, what is the potential role of numerical simulation within such a literature?

There has been a limited amount of theoretical work in which the presence of a "center," defined as a peaking of density, is not predetermined. There are two highly similar papers by Beckmann [30] and Borukhov and Hochman [34] which produce a circular city with high densities at the center and declining with distance from the center, under the assumption that each household interacts with every other household by means of social trips. The outcome of this analysis is a "monocentric" city which emerges without any predetermined employment center. In fact these models are purely residential in character and have no explicit or implicit employment activity. Their basic insight is that the presence of spatial interaction among the members of a homogeneous population is sufficient to produce monocentricity, where the center emerges as a peaking of density.

This basic insight has been taken one step further in a paper by Fujita and Ogawa [63] who introduce two internally homogeneous sectors (households and business firms) in a linear (constant width) uniform space without a predetermined center. Households choose their land use and their locations of work and residence but do not have any agglomerative social interaction with each other. Firms are competitive due to free entry and use the labor of the commuting households and of land, in fixed amounts, to produce a profit maximizing composite commodity output. The productivity of each firm is influenced also by an agglomerative effect which is a function of the density of surrounding firms.

The authors show numerically, the presence of multiple equilibria under each fixed set of parameter values. In particular, these patterns are: (a) monocentric configuration with firms in the center, (b) duocentric configurations (two concentrations of firms surrounded by residences), (c) the completely mixed configuration (without commuting), (d) the incompletely mixed configuration (a blend of (b) and (c)), and (e) the tricentric urban configuration.

Additional polycentric equilibria exist but are not examined by the authors. That these results need to be established numerically is significant given the relative simplicity of the model's assumptions.

Basically, the type of equilibrium, from those listed above, depends crucially on two parameter values. One of these is the parameter controlling the strength of the agglomeration effect and the other is the unit cost of commuting. For example (and in accordance with intuition) when the commuting unit cost is sufficiently high then the completely mixed pattern (c) is an equilibrium. The other patterns, showing various degrees of concentration occur as the agglomeration effect gets stronger relative to the unit commuting cost.

The authors use numerical simulation to explore patterns of structural change in urban form as the commuting cost varies or as the population level increases continuously. Starting with the completely mixed configuration they find that the urban form can undergo complex transitions. For example, decreasing the commuting rate continuously, the urban form changes to the incompletely mixed pattern continuously but after some critical value is reached, the urban form changes again but suddenly. Furthermore, such transitions are not always reversible by reversing the path of the exogenous parameters.

The Fujita and Ogawa paper thus demonstrates the importance of numerical simulation in multicentric urban economics, which is in its infancy. In particular, the contracts among firms need to be made explicit and embedded into production theory for such models of land use to be advanced further.

2. NON-ECONOMIC BEGINNINGS

Where there is the need, there is often the will and where there is the will there is the way. In this spirit, urban planners, some economists and non-economists from other scientific disciplines perceived the need to build large scale models of urban areas for forecasting and analyzing their structure and dynamics and for prescribing policy. As we discussed in the introduction, the lack of an accessible urban economic theory (which was also in its formative stage) was not perceived as a discouraging factor. Nor were there sufficient efforts to root these early models in alternative theoretical disciplines. The "will" came from the availability of the mathematics for large scale problems, the growing power of computers to solve such problems and the apparent availability of data to represent an urban area at various levels of disaggregation.

Even though an economic theory of cities did not assert itself strongly enough at that time, there was a widespread appreciation of what might be called the undergrowth out of which the theory was emerging. An urban *system* (rather than *economy*) was understood to be amenable to scientific explanation, mathematical representation and societal manipulation. It was fashionable in the fifties and sixties to view complex systems as highly subject to rational analysis. Urban areas with their rapid growth and many unsolved problems encouraged such a view. Unfortunately, when there is a "will" without a theory there is generally not one "way" but several "ways." Thus during the five year period from 1964 to 1969 four powerful models asserted themselves and had a major impact on the large number of urban scientists who were doing new thinking on how to build simulation models for an urban system.

In this part we will review these four models not in the chronological order of their emergence, nor in the order of the debate and excitement which they created at the time. Rather our review will use the benefit of hindsight which allows us to order these models according to their eventually realized impact and ultimate usefulness. Thus, Forrester's *Urban Dynamics* published in 1969 [56] was the least influential of these attempts, leading to no extensions whatsoever, even though at the time it might have appeared to some that it was preempting the entire future research agenda of urban economics. The second least influential attempt was Hill's EMPIRIC model [84]. It was applied widely but perhaps not very usefully. This model is so akin to input–output analysis in assumptions and mathematical structure that it could have flourished, one would have to assume, were it not for competition from Lowry's model [115] on the one hand and urban economic theory on the other. Lowry's model was successful and was extended in a number of applications which have continued to this day. The model was the only one in the group developed by an economist and although it remained completely divorced from urban economic theory it had enough structure to continue attracting attention.

Indirectly, Lowry's model inspired Wilson's maximum entropy model [185] which—more than a model—was a statistical theory of spatial interactions. This development spurred a new wave of improved Lowry-type models to emerge and become avidly applied in Britain and elsewhere.

2.1. Forrester's urban dynamics

Forrester's approach to building an urban model is rooted in a method of analysis which emerged in control engineering and discussed in Forrester's earlier books *Industrial Dynamics* [54] and *Principles of Systems* [55]. The method of analysis has led to a special computer language called DYNAMO put together by researchers at the Massachusetts Institute of Technology.

The logic of this approach hinges on the manipulation of three types of variables called *level, rate* and *auxiliary* variables. A level variable describes the state of the system at time t while a rate variable measures an increment (increase or decrease) in a level variable during a time period (for example from t to $t + 1$). An *auxiliary* variable can in turn determine a level or rate variable or another auxiliary variable but is not itself a rate or level variable of direct interest to be solved within the model. Level and rate variables are like *stock* and *flow* variables in econometric models and auxiliary variables are like *exogenous* variables or policy instruments as well as like *intermediate endogenous* variables. Putting these ingredients together, one may create a feedback loop within a Forrester-type model. For example, a level variable is changed for the next period by the influence of exogenous auxiliary variables on the associated rate variable. The rate variable is a function of another auxiliary variable which is in turn a function of the level thus creating a feedback. To build a complete model all one must do is to identify the variables in each category and write down the equations for each level and each rate and some auxiliary variables as functions of the other rate, level and auxiliary variables. This results in a number of simultaneous equations which must be solved recursively for each period and which may be decomposed into a number of separable systems linked only by some auxiliary variables.

Armed with the above panoply, Forrester bravely attempted a foray into the jungle of urban interactions. His objective was to examine the entire life cycle of an urban area from birth to growth and maturity and finally to stagnation. His model of the city consisted of 150 equations and was much reminiscent of his earlier attempt to model industrial dynamics [54]. The sheer size and complexity of Forrester's model makes it difficult to present an equation-by-equation description but to give a flavor of the scope and some of the model's structure, we can examine just how Forrester attempted to represent the underlying urban economy.

First of all Forrester's model is an aspatial model. In this respect it contrasts with all other models in urban economics. Thus, the relative location of industries and businesses within the urban area is not considered and there is no transportation sector. Secondly, there is a land supply available to the city which, however, remains fixed over the entire 250 year long simulation period.

The model has twelve sectors. Of these, three are what an economist would like to call housing markets: premium housing, worker housing and underemployed housing. Another three sectors represent labor markets for managers, laborers and underemployed laborers. A third group of three sectors represent firms or industries: new business, mature business and declining business. A tenth sector is government or public finance and an eleventh sector describes urban renewal and development programs. The twelfth and final sector consists of a number of identities, equilibrium conditions and other consistency relationships.

Although the model is not economic, it does make an effort to capture some phenomena previously recognized by urban economists as being important. For example, the labor market equtions do not in fact resemble labor supply and demand relationships. These equations deal with in-migration and out-migration of the three employee classes. Migration is a function of the perceived attractiveness of the city which is a lagged function of actual attractiveness, the latter depending on public services, available jobs, available housing and upward mobility to a higher labor class.

The housing sector models filtering of the stock downward among the housing classes. Public renewal programs can construct each type of stock but private construction occurs only for premium and worker housing. Construction is determined by lagged desired construction (presumably "demand") which depends on land availability, property taxes, employment growth and the adequacy of existing housing.

Similar to the above, a key feature of the business sector is that new businesses emerge as needed and mature and eventually become declining businesses which are demolished. The rates of transformation and demolition are endogenously determined. For example, new business construction depends on desired new business construction determined in part by a multiplier which depends on the availability of land, business taxes and classes of labor. Input–output type of coefficients determine the depletion of land by each type of housing and business.

Forreseter's dynamic simulations generally produce the following long term cycle: urban growth starts when the city is very small and gradually speeds up. After a long period of acceleration, deceleration occurs and eventually there is total stagnation. This cycle is almost entirely built in. Acceleration comes from the driving forces of migration which get bigger as new businesses increase attractiveness and also because new enterprise construction is an increasing function of the growth of new enterprises. Deceleration is inevitable because total land is fixed. Thus, Forrester's model may be applicable to a central city with legal boundaries but is certainly irrelevant for a metropolitan economy which in principle can claim much larger quantities of land from agriculture.

These and other structurally built-in biases in Forrester's model have been critized by economists and most notably by Mills [125; pp. 79, 80]. Mills discussed six policies examined by Forrester to ascertain their effectiveness in reducing stagnation. Four policies which do not work are (a) public sector job creation for the underemployed, (b) training program for the underemployed, (c) federal aid to the public sector, (d) low-cost housing program. These programs attract more underemployed into the city from an unlimited pool outside until the newcomers reduce land available for the higher classes and for industry, worsening the situation and increasing all stagnation indices. The policies that work well are (a) public new business construction, (b) demolition of slums and declining businesses. According to Mills, again, the reason these policies succeed is because there is no limit to the growth of industry to alleviate unemployment and reduce distress signals postponing stagnation. Certainly, it would have been possible to construct and numerically solve Forrester's model in such a way that the former policies succeeded and the latter failed. This property of Forrester's system makes his entire approach totally dependent on empirical justification which he does not provide and could hardly be provided for his large and complex model. Another problem is that the basic acceleration–deceleration–stagnation cycle can be obtained with a much simpler model since it derives unavoidably from the arbitrarily fixed land supply. Too many relationships are included in the model to obtain such an obvious result.

The model is not even superficially connected with economic theory. As Mills puts it [125; p. 80]:

It is hard to take Forrester's model seriously as a description of the urban economy. It contains no production functions except input–output coefficients for land and labor. It contains no factor prices and no factor markets that are recognizable to economists. It contains no output prices and no output markets. There are many ad hoc assumptions about lags, functional forms, and coefficient values. All are introduced without reference to economic theory or empirical studies. Although the model makes strong and implausible assumptions about migration, public finance, and urban labor markets, there is no indication that it has been influenced by previous work in any of these areas. Economists have not, of course, said the last word on any of these subjects, and there is no reason for Forrester to accept any specific results. But Forrester simply ignores everything economists have said about production, markets and public finance. He puts forward his own hypotheses without justification, as though their statement makes them self-evident, whereas the opposite is true.

This judgement on the Forrester model has been decisive and final as nothing more has been heard from the proponents of the approach. At this point in time it may not be entirely pointless to pause and ask if the Forrester approach does still have any relevance for economic urban stimulation. The answer may be a qualified "yes." What was appealing, though certainly not distinctly urban, about Forrester's approach was the complex interplay of sectors and the inherently dynamic nature of the underlying processes connected with lags and feedbacks. It is suggestive of a general disequilibrium model if only the equations of such a model could be derived from the microeconomic theory of markets and still conform to a stock-flow representation of the variables.

2.2. Hill's EMPIRIC model

In contrast with the Forrester model which ignored the locational aspects of urban dynamics, Hill in 1965 [84] developed a model intended to forecast differential impacts among the various zones *within* an urban area. The model was developed for the Boston area and since then has been applied to a number of areas to study primarily the impact of public investments in infrastructure on differential growth among the zones. Nearly all of these applications occurred in a consultant or public sector environment and are unpublished and poorly documented. In the original Boston study the purpose was to evaluate transport investment. In another EMPIRIC study, sewer expansion in Washington, D.C. was investigated and the model was also applied to Minneapolis-St. Paul, Denver, Winnipeg, Canada and the Puget-Sound regions among others.

The model's equtions take the following form:

$$X_i^k = \sum_j A_{ij} X_j^k + \sum_n b_{in} Z_n^k,$$

where k denotes the zone or subarea, X_i^k measures the value of the ith endogeneous variable for zone k and Z_n^k the value of the nth exogenous variable for zone k. The coefficients A_{ij} and b_{in} are to be determined empirically and obviously measure the effect of a unit change in the jth endogenous and nth exogenous variable on the ith endogenous variable. Both exogenous and endogenous variables may be defined as levels or as rates of change in the levels of a previous time period. In some versions of the model the endogenous variables are defined as the share of a zone in the total level of that variable. We may organize the coefficients into the matrices $A = [a_{ij}]$ and $B = [b_{ik}]$ and the variables into column vectors $\bar{X}^k$ and $\bar{Z}^k$ for each zone k. Then, the endogenous variables for any zone k can be forecasted, given the exogenous variables for that zone, by means of the equations,

$$\bar{X}^k = (I - A)^{-1} B \bar{Z}^k,$$

where I is the identity matrix. This is possible because A is a square matrix with order equal to the number of variables and the product vector $B\bar{Z}^k$ is of the same order. Also we must assume that $I - A$ is nonsingular (the inverse exists).

The model has several serious shortcomings. First, it is intended that the simultaneous equations of the model be estimated for the coefficients in A and B using two stage least squares or other appropriate techniques. This requires that the model be identified and that there be a sufficient number of zones to serve as observations in this estimation. In most applications the model's equations have not been estimated simultaneously. Second, zones do not interact in forecasting, the exogenous variables of each zone completely determining the endogenous variables of that zone. Third, there is no built-in property which assures that forecasts of the endogenous variables will not be negative where such values are meaningless, or where these variables measure zone shares, that these shares will add up to one. In fact, the share-interpretation of the X variables is totally inappropriate. An ad-hoc procedure is needed to adjust these forecasts so that they sum to a given total which then needs to be forecasted independently. In some applications of the EMPIRIC model such adjustment procedures have apparently been used.

The EMPIRIC model is rather void of substance or may be viewed as a general framework allowing variables to be selected and specified in a number of ways. Typically, the X variables are the levels, rates of change or shares of different land uses and activities (to be determined within the model) whereas the Z variables are levels or rates of change in exogeneous factors and in policy instruments. For example, Z variables may be levels of expenditure in various infrastructure investments over a five year period (by zone) and the X variables are then the land use and activity responses to such investments again over a given five year period. In the original application by Hill [84] the model was used to forecast future traffic levels in the Boston region.

The structure of the EMPIRIC model demonstrates clearly the inadequacy of a linear simultaneous equation system for modeling urban interactions consistently, emphasizing the need for a non-linear formulation. Lowry's model [115], published one year before Hill's, did in fact respond to this challenge in a way which even in retrospect appears path breaking.

2.3. Lowry's model and extensions

Both Forrester and Hill were attempting to straightjacket the urban economy into mathematical frameworks developed and tested in other contexts. In Forrester's case this was the framework of control engineering and in Hill's case the simple structure of linear equation systems. In this respect neither approach was scientific in spirit. Lowry's model [115] published in 1964 took much more careful note of the particulars of the urban economy and it can be said that the model was developed to *solve the problem* rather than a new problem discovered to solve an existing mathematical model.

Lowry's model was developed for the Pittsburgh Regional Planning Association. Lowry, an economist, pivoted his model on the central idea of economic base theory. At the macro level this theory recognized a fundamental driving force in the regional (or metropolitan) economy. The economy of a region was driven by export oriented (or basic) employment. An increase in this employment created demand for housing for the new laborers who also demanded goods and services produced and consumed locally. This demand in turn created new local employment jobs setting off a new cycle of housing and local employment increments. The successive increments converged to a new total to determine the population and total employment of the area after the initial basic employment growth.

Lowry attempted to recast the above process within a spatial context, determining not only the total growth which occurred but also where within the metropolitian area this growth would be distributed and in what way would such distribution be guided by "market" forces.

Lowry divided the 420 square mile Pittsburgh region into 456 zones of approximately one square mile in area and then proposed the following system of simultaneous equations and some added inequalities.

The area of land in each zone is stratified by the equation:

$$A_j = A_j^U + A_j^B + A_j^S + A_j^H$$

where

A_j = the total area of land in zone j (known),

A_j^U = the area of unusable land in zone j (known),

A_j^B = the area of land in zone j used by basic employment (known or predetermined),

A_j^S = the area of land in zone j used by service (local) employment (unknown).

A_j^H = the area of land in zone j used by housing (unknown).

The service (local employment) sector was stratified into several types of employment. For each of these, the total service employment required by the households is given by,

$$E^K = a^k N$$

where

E^k = the service employment in service group k (unknown),

N = the number of households in the region (unknown),

a^k = empirically determined constants.

The distribution of employment among the zones depended on the strength of the nearby "market," which in turn is a function of the number of adjacent households and employment centers. Lowry's distribution function was,

$$E_j^k = b^k \left[\sum_i \left(\frac{c^k N_i}{T_{ij}^k} \right) + d^k E_j \right]$$

where,

E_j^k = the amount of employment in service group k located in zone j (unknown),

N_i = the residential population (in households), of zone i (unknown),

T_{ij}^k = the trip difficulty factor for the journey from home to shop for type k service employment (known),

c^k and d^k = empirically determined constants measuring the importance of households and workplaces as origins for shopping trips to service employment locations,

b^k = an endogenously determined (unknown) scale factor adjusting the service employment in each zone to the regional total E^k such that,

$$E^k = \sum_j E_j^k.$$

From the distribution equation we can see Lowry's assumption that workplaces generated shopping trips only to destinations within the same zone.

The amount of land taken up by service jobs in a given zone is computed by,

$$A_j^S = \sum_k e^k E_j^k,$$

where e^k is an empirically derived constant of land requirement per employee.

The total employment in a zone is the sum of the basic and sevice employment in that zone. Thus,

$$E_j = E_j^B + \sum_k E_j^k,$$

where E_j^B, the basic employment, is exogenously given and known.

The total number of households in the region is a function of the total employment,

$$N = f \sum_j E_j$$

where f is an empirically determined regional household per employee factor. The number of households in each zone is a function of the accessibility of that zone to employment opportunities,

$$N_j = g \sum_i \frac{E_i}{T_{ij}},$$

where,

N_j = the number of households in zone j,

T_{ij} = the trip difficulty factor for the journey from home to work,

g = an endogenously determined scaling factor which ensures that total population is equal to the sum of zone populations, namely,

$$N = \sum_j N_j.$$

The functions $(T_{ij})^{-1}$ and $(T_{ij}^k)^{-1}$ are $(T_{ij})^{-1} = a d_{ij}^{-x}$ for work trips and $(T_{ij}^k)^{-1} = (\alpha_k - \beta_k d_{ij} + \gamma_k d_{ij}^2)^{-1}$ for shopping trips. Note that these are purely functions of travel distance, d_{ij}, and do not consider other factors such as travel time, travel cost or indices of attractiveness.

Lowry estimated the positive coefficients a and x associated with the trip difficulty factor of the journey to work by means of the following empirical procedure. He sampled a number of employment centers in Pittsburgh. Then, he classified the zones surrounding each center into roughly one-mile wide rings extending outward from the center. He then observed that the relative frequency of trips terminating at a center and originating at a ring, dropped as a function of the ring's distance from its center at some exponential rate. Curve fitting to this data yielded the values of a and x used in the trip difficulty factor for the journey to work. See Figure 2(a).

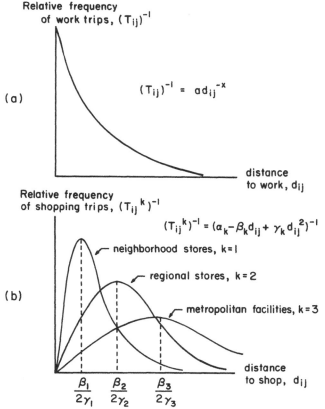

FIGURE 2   Lowry's empirically determined work-to-home and home-to-shop "trip difficulty" functions.

In the case of journey to shop Lowry dealt with a three-way classification of local or service employment. These were neighborhood stores, regional stores and metropolitan facilities. The scale of the typical establishment increased and the number to be found in a metropolitan area decreased as one went from the neighborhood to the regional to the metropolitan category. For example, barber stores, pharmacies and flower shops would be in the neighborhood category; department stores, hospitals, schools would be in the regional category and airports, public buildings, universities would be in the metropolitan category.

Lowry then proceeded to sample service employment zones and classify zones around them into rings. The relative frequency of shopping trips terminating at a shopping zone and originating at a ring first rose, peaked and then started falling exponentially with the ring's distance from the shopping employment. For neighborhood employment, peaking occurred rather quickly whereas for regional and metropolitan facilities the peak was found successively further away from the location of the employment. The peaking was a natural result of the customers' desire to drive a certain distance in search of higher quality shopping balanced against their dislike and cost of going too far away from home. Since regional and metropolitan facilities were located more sparsely than neighborhood facilities, the peaking occurred at distances further away from home locations. To these data Lowry fitted a quadratic equation estimating the coefficients α_k, β_k and γ_k for each type of shopping k. See Figure 2(b).

In the above system of equations, there are $JK + 4J + 2K + 2$ equations where J is the number of zones and K is the number of service employment types. The number of unknowns is the same and consists of E_j^k, A_j^S, A_j^H, E^k, N, N_j, E_j and the scale factors g and b^k. Given values for these scale factors, the simultaneous equations are linear in the remaining unknowns. In Lowry's case $J = 456$ and $K = 3$ so there were 3200 equations and unknowns.

One way ot obtain a solution of Lowry's model would be to fix g and b^k at some positive values and solve the remaining linear system. One would then adjust the values of g and b^k and repeat the above procedure until all equations were satisfied and all unknowns had positive values. This last requirement is a major problem with the Lowry model: if his system of equations has a solution it cannot be guaranted that all unknowns obtain positive values.

To be sure, Lowry's model had some additional features that helped him cirvumvent this problem of possibly negative allocations. He specified a number of inequalities. First, he noted that retail and other service outlets tended to cluster in groups, e.g. the suburban shopping center. This is reflected in the model by a constraint on the minimum amount of service employment, Z^k, in each zone. Then,

$$E_j^k \geq Z^k \quad \text{or} \quad E_j^k = 0.$$

Lowry also noted that the population of each zone is constrained to a maximum density Z_j^H (due to zoning ordinances or building technology constraints) which varies from zone to zone. Then,

$$N_j \leq Z_j^H A_j^H.$$

The constants Z^k and Z_j^H were given exogenously. This guaranteed that employment totals by zone will be nonnegative, but to guarantee that residential allocations are also nonnegative, Lowry had to employ the constraint

$$A_j^S \leq A_j - A_j^U - A_j^B,$$

a positive slack in this inequality being the quantity of the zone's land allocated to housing.

The major shortcomings of Lowry's Pittsburgh model are the following:

1) The simultaneous equations are linear in all the unknowns except the scale factors g and b^k. Assuming that a unique solution exists for all the unknowns (including the scale factors), such a solution can be infeasible if it does not fall within the feasible set defined by the inequality constraints. Thus, in possibly many cases, the Lowry model does not have a solution. Apparently many scholars who worked on extending the Lowry model are unaware of this problem.

2) The equations which distribute service employment and households do not admit a clear behavioral interpretation. In particular, the scale factors g and b^k remain uninterpretable. It is not clear *what* changes in their values represent. Here, the imagination of the reader must supplement the model.

3) The only variable which "explains" the distribution of households and service employment is the distance between zones. In the original Lowry model this was taken to be airline distance as opposed to a distance measure defined over a travel network. In some later extensions, this variable has been replaced by travel time, cost or both of these variables.

4) The equilibration of the demand for land (housing and employment) with the supply of land does not follow behavioral principles of supply–demand equilibrium, since the price variables needed to do this are not in the equations.

5) The land consumption coefficients and trip generation rates could be determined within the model but are either ignored by becoming absorbed into the scale factors or are given fixed values.

6) The model does not produce any measures of consumer or supply-side benefits.

The above points of criticism add up to the judgement that the model is not economic but physicalistic in nature: it allocates physical quantities such as jobs, households etc. without any regard to the prices which resolve such an allocation process in real markets.

Extensions of the Lowry model have made efforts to mitigate some of the above shortcomings. A popular modification is to replace the nonbehavioral trip difficulty factors with relative frequencies which have the form of the multinomial logit model. Thus,

$$P_{ij} = \frac{A_j f(d_{ij})}{\sum_n A_n f(d_{in})}$$

where A_j is a measure of the residential attractivenesss of zone j, $f(.)$ is an impedance function of the distance between i and j (such as travel cost and time) and P_{ij} is the proportion of the workers employed in i who choose zone j for residence. A similar relative frequency function is usually defined for the distribution of shopping trips from the place of residence. Such an approach was first taken in Goldner's [67] Projective Land Use Model (PLUM) which was a direct extension of Lowry's model. The zonal attractiveness measures are themselves functions of vacant developable, land, presence of sewer capacity, the numbers of various household types, other land uses already in the zone and other variables. This approach improves the appearance and detail of the distribution functions but does nothing to achieve consistent equilibration since the equilibrating price variables are still lacking from these models. Equilibration in these models is forced and inconsistent. It is achieved by imposing arbitrary distributional assumptions in allocating the initially computed excess demands.

Although Lowry was an economist operating without a theory of space and the urban economy, perhaps all who extended the Lowry model are noneconomists. This may be because the seminal contributions which introduced urban economic theory were published at the same year or within a few years of Lowry's model, thereafter capturing the attention of economists. Another possible reason is that the work of Wilson [185], to be discussed next, greatly enhanced the consistency of Lowry type models but from a statistical, noneconomic point-of-view inspiring Lowry type models which became widely used in Britain and elsewhere. For coverage of these developments the reader may consult the book by Batty [24].

At the substantive level, Lowry's Pittsburgh model raised a number of interesting questions that have not yet been investigated empirically with improved economic models. If the number of jobs in basic employment in Pittsburgh were to be increased, would this result in the formation of new shopping center concentrations in the long run or in a reinforcement of the existing number and location of shopping centers? What was the long term share of the downtown in the region's total employment level? How should basic employment be zoned or distributed within the metropolis to achieve a desired pattern or expansion for the metropolis?

At the technical level the Lowry Model created great enthusiasm in the ability of the computer to solve urban simulation models and to produce quick tangible forecases. This enthusiasm was so strong that it detracted attention from the more important job of improving the mathematical and behavioral formulation of Lowry's model.

Urban modelers were by and large content to write computer programs which were presented as black boxes. As long as these tools could produce and print out certain forecasts they were considered immune from any scrutiny into their mathematical form. Perhaps the most noteworthy example of this view is the work of

Putman [138] who nearly three decades after the original Lowry model continues in this tradition.

2.4. Wilson's entropy principle and discrete choice models

The problem which is perhaps most characteristic of transportation planning is the so called "trip distribution problem." According to this problem we wish to estimate the number of trips that will occur between various zone pairs (i, j) given that we know the number of trips originating and terminating in each zone. For example, let O_i be the number of work trips originating in zone i because of a given supply of jobs there and let D_i be the number of work trips terminating at zone i because of a given trip generating capacity tied to the number of dwellings there. Given these numbers for every zone $i = 1 \ldots I$ what is the number of trips N_{ij} that is most likely to occur between zone i and zone j? For feasibility we assume

$$\sum_i O_i = \sum_i D_i = N \quad \text{and, of course,} \quad \sum_i \sum_j N_{ij} = N.$$

An old way of solving this problem is the gravity model which is of the form

$$N_{ij} = G_{ij} \frac{O_i D_j}{d_{ij}^2},$$

and corresponds to Newton's gravity law with d_{ij} the distance between i and j and with the values of the G_{ij}'s adjusted to assure that the trip distribution satisfies the marginals $\sum_i N_{ij} = D_j$ and $\sum_j N_{ij} = O_i$. Of course, if we are free to choose each G_{ij} then it is easy to satisfy these marginal conditions. A more interesting form of the problem defines $G_{ij} = A_i B_j$ where A_i and B_j are "balancing factors." It is known that these can be found so that a unqiue trip matrix of N_{ij}'s satisfies the marginals. It is also common to replace the square-of-distance term with a more general increasing function of distance $f(d_{ij})$.

The history of the gravity model is too far removed from urban economics to be of interest to us but it suffices to say that variants of it have been applied to trip distribution ever since the 1940's and 1950's and through most of the 1960's. It was in 1967 when Wilson [185] provided a statistical interpretation of the gravity model via his entropy or minimum information principle. What Wilson did was to prove that a generalized gravity model is in fact the most probable prediction of trips possible under some given information. Wilson's notion of probability is based on a combinatorial reasoning. If we know the total number of trips N and all the states of the system (i, j) and if we have no information about any of the individual trip markers, then the most probable trip distribution matrix $\{N_{ij}\}$ is that which can be realized by the largest number of ways of assigning the N individuals to the given states (zone pairs) such that some observed aggregate constraints on this distribution are satisfied. The number of ways (permutations) that will yield the matrix $\{N_{ij}\}$ may be denoted as $W\{N_{ij}\}$ and is

$$W\{N_{ij}\} = N! \Big/ \prod_{i,j} N_{ij}!.$$

Taking the natural logarithm of this we get

$$\ln W\{N_{ij}\} = \ln(N!) - \sum_{i,j} \ln(N_{ij}!)$$

and for N_{ij} large, we may use Stirling's approximation

$$\ln(N_{ij}!) \simeq N_{ij} \ln N_{ij}.$$

Then, ignoring the constant $\ln(N!)$, a measure of the probability of a trip matrix $\{N_{ij}\}$ is the entropy of the trip matrix

$$E = - \sum_{i,j} N_{ij} \ln N_{ij}.$$

This entropy is monotonically related to Shannon's or Theil's measure of information (see Shannon and Weaver [149], Theil [168]). This measure is based on the notion that the information content of an event is equal to minus one times the natural logarithm of the probability (or relative frequency) of the event. Thus, an event which is certain to occur contains no surprise and is therefore totally uninformative, whereas an event with a probability of occurrence nearly zero (if it occurs) is infinitely surprising and informative. Then, the expected information in our probability or relative frequency distribution is:

$$T = - \sum P_{ij} \ln P_{ij},$$

where P_{ij} is the relative frequency of trips choosing state (i, j) or $P_{ij} = N_{ij}/N$. Making this substitution we can verify that the information of the relative frequency distribution and the entropy of the trip matrix are related by

$$T = \frac{E}{N} - \ln N.$$

More precisely, Shannon's measure is the expected level of information in the relative frequency distribution. This follows if $\ln P_{ij}$ is defined as the information associated with the (i, j)th state. Suppose that $P_{ij} = 1$ and $P_{km} = 0$ for all $(k, m) \neq (i, j)$. In this case we have a deterministic probability (or relative frequency) distribution. Shannon's measure for this case obtains the value zero, which is the lowest possible value for it: a deterministic distribution is uninformative because it contains no surprises. Another distribution we may consider is the uniform distribution. In our case all $P_{ij} = P = 1/I^2$. Such a distribution contains the highest possible level of information which is, in our case, $2 \ln I$.

Equipped with this notion of entropy or the perfectly equivalent notion of Shannon's information, Wilson was able to ask the crucial question: assuming that there are constraints that can be imposed on a distribution (or trip matrix) what is the most probable (i.e. most random) or most informative distribution that will satisfy those constraints? To find the answer one can maximize the entropy E subject to the constraints or one can equivalently minimize $-T$ subject to equivalent constraints. We will choose the second method or presentation. Then, Wilson's problem is,

$$\underset{\{P_{ij}\}}{\text{Minimize}} \sum_{i,j} P_{ij} \ln P_{ij}$$

subject to:

$$\sum_i P_{ij} = D_j/N; \qquad j = 1 \ldots J,$$

$$\sum_j P_{ij} = O_i/N; \qquad i = 1 \ldots I,$$

$$\sum_{ij} P_{ij} X_{ijk} = X_k/N; \qquad k = 1 \ldots K.$$

The meaning of imposing these constraints on the relative frequency distribution may be explained as follows. First, if this distribution is to be unbiased, it ought to replicate the observed marginal totals of the matrix of trips. Second, supposing that there are $k = 1 \ldots K$ characteristics (or attributes) which obtain the values X_{ijk} for the (i, j)th state, then an unbiased relative frequency distribution should replicate the average observed value of each to these attributes. In Wilson's statement of this problem the notion of "bias" was not the motivating criterion nor is it necessary to interpret the constraints in this way. This is simply better econometrician's language. Also, in Wilson's original statement of the problem, $K = 1$ and this single attribute considered was travel cost.

The problem is one with a strictly convex objective function and linear constraints. It can be solved by forming the Lagrangian with multipliers λ_i and θ_j to correspond to the ith and jth origin and destination constraints respectively and β_k to correspond to the kth attribute constraint. The unique solution has the form,

$$P_{ij} = \frac{\exp(\sum_k \beta_k X_{ijk} + \lambda_i + \theta_j)}{\sum_{m,n} \exp(\sum_k \beta_k X_{mnk} + \lambda_m + \theta_n)}.$$

This is the multinomial logit model in which the Lagrangian multipliers appear as coefficients and are unrestricted in sign. The β_k's obtain unique values and λ_i's and θ_j's are obtained in such a way that the marginal constraints are satisfied and the β_k's are obtained so that the attribute constraints are satisfied.

Now the gravity model with which we started this subsection is a very special form of the multinomial logit model in which $K = 1$ and $X_{ij1} = \ln d_{ij}$ where d_{ij} is the distance between i and j and $\beta_1 = -2$. Also, $G_{ij} = A_i B_j$ where

$$A_i = 1 \bigg/ \sum_j B_j D_j \exp(-2 \ln d_{ij})$$

and

$$B_j = 1 \bigg/ \sum_i A_i O_i \exp(-2 \ln d_{ij}).$$

The λ_i's and θ_j's do not appear because their role has been taken over by the A_i's and B_j's. For the proof see Anas [5].

In this way Wilson was able to provide a statistical theory for the gravity model and, more importantly, for a wide range of distribution functions such as those implied in Lowry's model, for example.

The economic interpretation of the multinomial logit model did not come until 1974 when McFadden [121] rederived it from utility maximization. In this derivation, adapted to our context, we postulate a utility function

$$U_{ij} = \sum_k \beta_k X_{ijk} + \lambda_i + \theta_j + \varepsilon_{ij}$$

for the state (i, j) which is now treated as a discrete choice alternative. In other words, each tripmaker is treated as a decision maker who is to choose one of the I^2 origin-destination pairs. In our example this may mean choosing a place of work *and* a place of residence. The utility of each origin destination pair is evaluated on the basis of the K attributes with marginal utilities β_k and two origin and destination specific constant utility terms. The final part ε_{ij} is a random disturbance which varies among the N decision makers. It is typically assumed that ε_{ij} obtains a deterministic value for each decision maker but that this value is not observed by the analyst (or econometrician). Then, it is assumed that each ε_{ij} is Gumbel distributed independently and identically over the population of decision makers. Thus,

$$\text{Prob}(\varepsilon_{ij} \le \varepsilon) = \exp(-\exp(-\varepsilon)).$$

With these assumptions, stochastic utility maximization from

$$P_{ij} = \text{Prob}[U_{ij} > U_{mn}; \quad (m, n) \ne (i, j)],$$

yields the multinomial logit model independently derived by Wilson [185] from entropy maximization.

McFadden [121] proposed that the utility coefficients (which correspond to the Lagrangian multipliers in Wilson's problem as shown by Anas [5]) be estimated by maximizing the likelihood that the observed choices are predicted by the multinomial logit model. This estimation method apparently required that the actual choices of the decision makers be observed. In our problem, let $\overset{\circ}{n}_{ij}$ be the number of decision makers observed to choose (i, j), then the likelihood function to be maximized for the coefficients $\bar{\beta}$, $\bar{\lambda}$ and $\bar{\theta}$ is,

$$L = \frac{N!}{\prod_{i,j} \overset{\circ}{n}_{ij}!} \prod_{i,j} P_{ij}(\bar{\beta}, \bar{\lambda}, \bar{\theta})^{\overset{\circ}{n}_{ij}},$$

where $P_{ij}(\bar{\beta}, \bar{\lambda}, \bar{\theta})$ is the multinomial logit model. Anas [5] proved that the estimates of the coefficients obtained from this likelihood maximization are precisely the same as those obtained from entropy maximization with the same data. This implies the corrollary that the actual choices $\{\overset{o}{n}_{ij}\}$ which are not used in entropy maximization need not be observed, even though they deceptively appear in the likelihood function. The proof is rather simple. It requires only to show that the first order conditions of the likelihood maximization correspond precisely to the first order conditions of the entropy maximizing problem and that the actual choices $\{\overset{o}{n}_{ij}\}$ appear in these equations only in aggregated form.

The statistical properties of likelihood maximization for the multinomial logit model have been examined by McFadden [121] who proved that the coefficients and the choices predicted from them are asymptotically unbiased and efficient.

Another result established by Williams [184] and later generalized by Small and Rosen [155] is that in a multinomial logit model the expression

$$\frac{1}{\alpha} \ln \sum_{m,n} \exp \left\{ \sum_{k} \beta_k X_{mnk} + \lambda_m + \theta_n \right\},$$

(where α is the marginal utility of income) is the consumer surplus. The rest of the expression is the expected maximum utility over the available choices.

The equivalence between McFadden's multinomial logit model and the same model obtained independently by Wilson is of considerable interest because the work of these two scholars had inspired quite different and competitive schools of research. Followers of Wilson have used these models with relatively little interest in their econometric specification giving rise to an extensive school of aggregative models intended to solve Lowry type problems. A book which reviews this literature and partakes in its style of reasoning has been written by Batty [24]. Followers of McFadden, on the other hand, have been primarily interested in estimating discrete choice models (logit, nested logit [122] and probit [39]) in various contexts giving rise to a very lively branch of applied econometrics. Some such applications within urban economics, or closely related to it, are on travel demand by Domencich and McFadden [47]; on housing demand by Quigley [140], Ellickson [49]; joint travel and location demand by Lerman [110], Anas [4], Anas and Chu [10]; the location of firms by Carlton [37], Miller and Lerman [123]; the choices by landlords and developers by Anas [4, Ch. 4; 6]. Econometricians following McFadden have been less interested in building aggregative simulation models with discrete choice equations. Recently, however, there has been two such developments: one is in the area of housing market models by Anas [4] to be reviewed in part four of this article and the other in the area of stochastic choice of route in urban travel by Daganzo and Sheffi [40] to be discussed in the next part. These two lines of research suggest that Lowry–Wilson type models have now been unified with economic theory and econometrics and that they will probably continue to inspire future applied work in simulation modeling. Recently, Anas and Cho [8] identified some general conditions for establishing the existence and uniqueness of equilibrium prices in such models constructed from discrete choice theory.

At this point, it is useful to reflect on how spatial equilibrium models of the urban economy based on discrete choice theory can replace the deterministic models of the monocentric tradition for realistic policy analysis. The case for this has been made in the book by Anas [4]. The chief advantage of these models is that they admit taste heterogeneity. The monocentric literature pretends that the urban population of firms or households can be divided into distinct and internally homogeneous classes. This is not only impossible in empirical practice but should also be distasteful in theory. No matter what market segmentation variables one might use, a residual amount of hetenogeneity *within* each segment is unavoidable. No two market actors are clones of each other. A group of market actors who are seemingly identical because of strong similarity in several key attributes can and do behave in diverse ways in the marketplace due to random factors. No city is divided into distinct and internally homogeneous areas. Rather, each area exhibits diversity and heterogeneity to some degree and in some variables. The choices of seemingly similar market actors exhibit wide dispersion. Discrete choice models capture these empirical regularities and provide a basis for revamping the extreme homogeneity assumption of monocentric theory. Paradoxically discrete choice models provide a demonstration that econometrics, wherein these models originated, can be a good place for initiating a new breed of theoretical analysis, that proves to be more realistic, more flexible and more applicable than the old. Econometric models rooted in discrete choice theory (see Anas [4]) are discussed in more detail in Section 4. Computationally, these models are very tractable and the excess demand functions can be solved using various iterative search techniques. Furthermore, since there are no "borders" between land uses that must be computed, the computational procedure is direct. Anas [4; Ch. 5] reports such computational experience with a model in which there are nearly 1700 excess demand equations. The cost is minimal and the simulations show the dispersal of the choices of each market segment and the resulting mixture of market segments at each location.

3. MATHEMATICAL PROGRAMMING

The models reviewed in this part have two characteristics in common. One is that they all rely on mathematical programming as a means of formulation. The other is that although these models can be used as predictive (or forecasting) tools their major usefulness is normative since they constitute frameworks for examining the correspondence between market equilibrium and optimum. Thus, they provide a basis for evaluating market failure and the efficiency of resource allocation. The relationship between equilibrium and optimum was examined in part one in the context of monocentric urban land use models but the models discussed in this part make generalizations to the context of a realistic zonal representation of an urban area.

The models we are about to discuss have been used or are being used as forecasting tools with various degrees of success and empirical sophistication. They hold a great deal of promise for future implementations which could no doubt emerge as the power of computers to solve large scale mathematical programming problems continues to improve.

We will first discuss traffic network equilibrium models the purpose of which is to forecast the flow of traffic on an urban road network. These are perhaps the most routinely utilized class of large scale models in existence and they have achieved wide acceptance in transportation planning agencies despite their very crude assumptions which will be demonstrated to be inconsistent with steady state flow. Spatial price equilibrium models, originated by Samuleson [145], are considered as simple variants of the traffic equilibrium problem because they are similar mathematically. Next we consider transport network design models the purpose of which is to determine the optimal configuration of a traffic network within an urban area. These problems quickly reach an extraordinary level of combinatorial complexity and exact or approximate (heuristic) solutions become difficult to obtain. As a result, these models have only been applied to stylized small network examples for purposes of research.

The linear programming models of Herbert and Stevens [83] and Mills–Hartwick [124, 76] solve problems of urban location and land use under various assumptions. Their empirical application to real problems or to forecasting has been only partial and fraught with some difficulties. Yet, these models are still appealing and can be expected to receive more future attention.

The Koopmans–Beckmann [105] problem provided the basis for interesting questions regarding the allocation of indivisible facilities but contains two characteristics which impede its application. One of these is the rather unrealistic assumptions it makes about spatial interaction and the other is the great computational cost that is encountered when this model is applied to large problems.

3.1. Traffic network and spatial price equilibrium models

Prediction of traffic flows on an urban road network is the transportation planner's technical problem *par excellence*. In order to understand the nature of this problem we must first discuss the mathematical representation of a traffic network. First, the urban area is divided into *zones* which serve as the origins and/or destinations of trips. Trips originating from or terminating in a zone are loaded onto or unloaded from a network at various *nodes* of the network connected to each other by network *links*. A network link is an aggregation of actual urban roads and the entire link–node network is thus an abstract aggregation of the actual urban road network. An origin-destination pair is connected by a large number of *routes* each of which is a sequence of links that can be traveled from that origin to that destination. To keep track of the member-ship of links to routes and routes to origin-destination pairs we define R_{ij} to be the set of routes connecting origin destination pair (i, j) and we define zero-one variables such that

$$a_{ij}^{l\rho} = \begin{cases} 1 & \text{if } l \in \rho \in R_{ij} \\ 0, & \text{otherwise.} \end{cases}$$

Here $l = 1 \ldots L$ are the links of the network and ρ represents a route.

The key difficulty in traffic equilibrium is the presence of congestion. The travel time (or "generalized *average cost* of travel") on link l is c_l and this is assumed to be an increasing and usually strictly convex function of the *total* traffic flow, f_l, on link l. Thus,

$$c_l = g_l(f_l) \quad \text{with} \quad g_l'(\ . \ ) > 0 \quad \text{and} \quad g_l(\ . \ ) > 0.$$

There are now two key computations. The first is the cost of a route $\rho \in R_{ij}$. It is simply the sum of the costs of traveling each link on the route. Thus,

$$c_{ij\rho} = \sum_l a_{ij}^{l\rho} g_l(f_l).$$

The second computation is finding the flow on a link. This is done by summing over all routes having that link in common. Thus, let $X_{ij\rho}$ be the number of trips on route $\rho \in R_{ij}$, then

$$f_l = \sum_{i,j,\rho \in R_{ij}} a_{ij}^{l\rho} X_{ij\rho}.$$

The concept of equilibrium in traffic flow was apparently first discussed by Knight [104] in 1924. Wardrop [172] in 1952 actually stated the equilibrium conditions explicitly and these are now known as the "Wardrop conditions" or "Wardrop's user-optimal conditions." What Wardrop suggested was that each traveler takes the least cost route available for travel. At equilibrium, this implies that all routes connecting an origin-destination pair and carry some traffic from that origin to that destination have the same cost and all routes which carry no traffic from that origin to that destination do not have a lower cost. This results in an equilibrium cost of travel from each origin to each destination.

In 1956, Beckmann, McGuire and Winsten [31] more clearly formulated the concept of traffic equilibrium and proposed (but did not solve numerically) a convex programming problem and thus proved the existence and uniqueness of traffic flows on a network. These authors realized that for equilibrium to be sustained on a network it is necessary that the equilibrium costs generated by route choices must be such that the trips (demand) generated from these costs are precisely such as to create those same costs. It is clear that this principle must hold at equilibrium for *each route* as well as *each link* on the network. We shall see below that this assumption is almost never satisfied everywhere on a real network.

The convex programming problem of Beckmann *et al.* [31] can be stated as follows:

$$\underset{\{\bar{X}, \bar{d}\}}{\text{minimize}} \sum_l \int_0^{f_l} g_l(s)\, ds - \sum_{i,j} \int_0^{d_{ij}} D_{ij}^{-1}(s)\, ds$$

subject to:

$$f_l = \sum_{i,j,\rho \in R_{ij}} a_{ij}^{l\rho} X_{ij\rho}; \quad \text{each } l,$$

$$\sum_{\rho \in R_{ij}} X_{ij\rho} \geq d_{ij}; \quad \text{each } (i, j),$$

$$X_{ij\rho} \geq 0; \quad \text{each } (i, j, \rho).$$

Here, the new notation, d_{ij}, is the number of trips between origin–destination pair (i, j) generated from the travel demand function, $D_{ij}(\min_{\rho \in R_{ij}} c_{ij\rho})$ for the origin–destination pair (i, j). Using the Kuhn–Tucker theorem, Beckmann *et al.* [31] proved that the unique equilibrium solution to the above convex programming problem implies Wardrop's conditions and thus generates equilibrium traffic assignments. These conditions are stated as follows:

a) if $X_{ij\rho} > 0$, $\rho \in R_{ij}$; then

$$c_{ij\rho} = c_{ij} = D_{ij}^{-1}(d_{ij}); \qquad \sum_{\rho \in R_{ij}} X_{ij\rho} = d_{ij}$$

b) if $X_{ij\rho} = 0$, $\rho \in R_{ij}$; then

$$c_{ij\rho} \geq c_{ij} = D_{ij}^{-1}(d_{ij}); \qquad \sum_{\rho \in R_{ij}} X_{ij\rho} = d_{ij},$$

where c_{ij} is the cost of travel from i to j at equilibrium. The network equilibrium problem can also be solved with fixed demands in which case each d_{ij} is given and the second term in the objective function can be dropped. The standard method used to solve this fixed demand network equilibrium problem is to apply the algorithm of Frank and Wolfe [57] which is applicable to a broader class of problems in operations research and was published coincidentally in 1956, the same year Beckmann *et al.* published the problem formulation. Various versions of this algorithm have been applied to the network problem, some with convergent results. The best known empirical applications of the problem to real networks are by Florian and Nguyen [53] to Winnipeg and by Eash, Janson and Boyce [48] to Chicago.

An issue of importance to economists is the relationship between the network equilibrium problem of traffic assignment and the optimal assignment which minimizes total transportation cost. The optimal assignment problem requires that the cost integrals in the objective function be replaced by the summation $\sum_l f_l g_l(f_l)$. Since congestion is an externality, the two problems differ in solution. The optimal solution can be decentralized, however, if each traveler is levied a congestion toll which link-by-traveled-link extracts the full marginal social cost of that traveler. Thus, in such a decentralized solution, network equilibrium follows again Wardrop's conditions except that now each traveler pays the average (private) cost as before plus a congestion toll which brings the total cost paid by the traveler to equal the traveler's marginal cost. In an elastic demand formulation, such marginal cost pricing reduces the total amount of travel on the network. Transportation planners have been aware of the optimal assignment problem (which they call *system optimal* assignment) and the relationship of this problem to the network equilibrium problem (which they call the *user optimal* assignment). However, transportation planners are generally uninterested in solving for optimal assignments, since congestion tolls are quite impractical to levy and also because they are not sufficiently interested in questions of efficiency. This is to be contrasted to the deep attention afforded to this topic by economists in a monocentric city context (see Section 1.2).

An important variation of the network equilibrium problem can be obtained by relaxing the assumption that all travelers perceive the same travel cost structure. Allowing random differences in perceived route travel costs one can formulate route choice as a problem in discrete choice thus deriving a multinomial probit or logit model of route choice. The approach was first suggested by Daganzo and Sheffi [40]. As an example, a multinomial logit model of route choice would specify the probability of choosing route $\rho \in R_{ij}$ as

$$P_{ij\rho} = \left(\frac{X_{ij\rho}}{d_{ij}}\right) = \frac{\exp\{\beta \sum_l a_{ij}^{l\rho} g_l(f_l)\}}{\sum_{s \in R_{ij}} \exp\{\beta_l \sum a_{ij}^{ls} g_l(f_l)\}},$$

where $\beta(<0)$ is the marginal disutility of travel cost.

The stochastic network equilibrium can now be obtained by solving the following fixed point problem where the probability functions $P_{ij\rho}(\bar{f})$ are the above multinomial logit model.

The fixed point problem is,

$$f_l - \sum_{i,j,\rho \in R_{ij}} a_{ij}^{l\rho} d_{ij} P_{ij\rho}(\bar{f}) = 0,$$

for each $l = 1 \ldots L$. These equations can be solved for the vector of equilibrium link flows, $\bar{f}$. Clearly, in the stochastic case each route in each set R_{ij} carries some traffic and this traffic generates congested costs which give rise to it. In the above formulation, the origin to destination demands d_{ij} are fixed.

An alternative method for obtaining the logit model of route choice was proposed by Fisk [52] and relies on entropy maximization. This formulation is,

$$\underset{(\bar{X},\bar{f})}{\text{minimize}} \sum_{i,j,\rho \in R_{ij}} X_{ij\rho} \ln X_{ij\rho}$$

subject to:

$$f_l - \sum_{i,j,\rho \in R_{ij}} a_{ij}^{l\rho} X_{ij\rho} = 0; \qquad \text{each } l,$$

$$\sum_l \int_0^{f_l} g_l(s)\, ds = \bar{C};$$

$$X_{ij\rho} \geq 0; \qquad \text{each } (i, j, \rho).$$

The result of this minimization is precisely the logit model of stochastic route choice which we saw above with β the Lagrangian multiplier of the integral constraint. $\bar{C}$ is the observed value of the left hand side of this constraint. It can be evaluated by using observed link flow values.

Anas [7] shows that the value of β estimated as the Lagrangian multiplier in Fisk's problem [52] is biased in comparison to the value of β in the logit model of stochastic route choice which could be estimated by applying maximum likelihood to that model. Thus, when there is congestion the equivalence between entropy maximization and likelihood maximization breaks down. Anas [7] also shows, however, that the equivalence is fully reestablished if the multinomial logit model of route choice is respecified to include a full set of link specific constants.

Thus,

$$P_{ij\rho} = \left(\frac{X_{ij\rho}}{d_{ij}}\right) = \frac{\exp\{\beta \sum_l a_{ij}^{l\rho}[g_l(f_l) + \theta_l]\}}{\sum_{s \in R_{ij}} \exp\{\beta \sum_l a_{ij}^{ls}[g_l(f_l) + \theta_l]\}},$$

where $\bar{\theta}$ are the link specific constants to be estimated together with β. With this formulation the entropy and likelihood methods yield the same asymptotically unbiased estimates of β and $\bar{\theta}$.

Despite substantial interest in stochastic route choice in recent years, such models have not yet been estimated and large stochastic network equilibrium problems have not been solved, even though such models appear to be much more realistic empirically than their deterministic counterparts. For some toy network solutions see Sheffi [150].

Having reviewed the literature, I must now reluctantly pull the rug from under it by exposing a fundamental inconsistency and ambiguity in the assumptions of steady state traffic flow embedded in these models. The inconsistency is as old as the original Beckmann *et al.* [31] book that initiated the literature, but in the three decades that have elapsed no one else seems to be perturbed by it, at least judging from the printed word.

To see the problem we will focus on the four simple networks of Figure 3. In network (a) there is a single link connecting a home location, H, with a workplace, W. Suppose that f trips originate at H and arrive at W. Clearly for each trip to have the same travel time on the link $H - W$ we could assume that they depart from H and arrive at W simultaneously. The travel time is $c = g(f)$. In network (b) there are two home locations $H1$ and $H2$ emitting f_1 and f_2 trips respectively and one workplace W that receives these trips. Because links 1 and 2 are not of the same length, to arrive at W at the same time the trips from $H2$ must depart just early enough to "catch" the trips from $H1$ at the juncture of 1, 2 and 3.

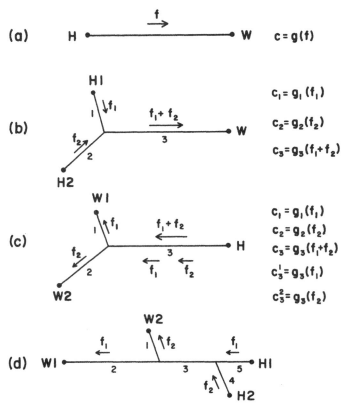

FIGURE 3   Four example networks.

Thereafter the trips $f_1 + f_2$ flow together on 3. The travel times are $c_1 = g_1(f_1)$, $c_2 = g_2(f_2)$ and $c_3 = g_3(f_1 + f_2)$. Note that if the two sets of trips did not arrive at W simultaneously then the above time computations for link 3 are meaningless. In that case there should be two *different* costs prevailing on link 3 at different times during the travel process.

In network (c) there is a single home location, H, but two workplaces $W1$ and $W2$ at different travel distances from H. In this case simultaneous arrival at $W1$ and $W2$ of the trips originating at H would require different departure times for those going from H to $W1$ from those going from H to $W2$. The literature computes the time on link 3 as $c_3 = g(f)$ where $f = f_1 + f_2$ is all the trips (or trips per hour) originating at H. This, of course is inconsistent. Two times prevail on link 3. Of these $c_3^1 = g_3(f_1)$ is the time for those going from H to $W2$ with f_1, f_2 the respective trips and $f_1 + f_2 = f$. Clearly, c_3 can greatly overestimate c_3^1 and c_3^2. To save the time computation assumptions of the literature for network (c) we must assume simultaneous departure from H but different arrival times at $W1$ and $W2$. In the case of network (d) neither simultaneous departure from homes nor simultaneous arrivals at work saves the computation for link 3. The proof is left as an exercise for the reader. To summarize, *the network equilibrium models compute link times as if all trips using a link use it simultaneously* or *as if there is an infinite reservoir of trips at each origin departing at the same rate per unit time.* This is a physical impossibility for even some simple arbitrary networks. To put it another way, it is easy to construct simple networks such that the link times, as computed in the network equilibrium literature, cannot occur under *any* systematic departure–arrival pattern. Certainly there is no reason for travelers to adjust their arrival–departure times so as to satisfy the link time computations of the traffic network equilibrium problem. Rather, arrival–departure timing decisions must be modeled in order to properly compute travel times on links *at different times* during the travel process.

Traffic flow on *networks* is an inherently dynamic process which involves *movement in space*. In such a problem neither "time" nor "space" can be collapsed. Beckmann, Winsten and McGuire [31] collapsed time which has led to the above inconsistency, and a flourishing literature that still ignores this inconsistency by claiming that traffic in these models flows at "steady state". It is clear from networks (c) and (d) of Figure 3 that steady state times cannot prevail as computed in the literature because the reservoir of trips at each origin is finite.

One way to put the literature back on the right rack is to develop dynamic models of traffic congestion. This work is in its infancy. Ben-Akiva, de Palma and Kanaroglou [32] have recently developed such a model for a simple network of two parallel links in which congestion is assumed to occur only at *fixed* bottleneck points (say highway ramps) but not on the links. Their model focuses on departure and arrival times as the choice variables of travelers and derives a distribution of these times during the peak period. The model is difficult to generalize to realistic networks.

Another challenge to the standard model came from Horowitz [87] who demonstrated by simulation that the "network equilibrium" is unstable for a simple two (parallel) link network, in which travellers can choose their route of travel.

Spatial price equilibrium problems were initiated by Samuelson [145] who investigated the clearing of spatially separated supply and demand markets. Given fixed transportation cost between various points in space (for example, cities or regions or points within an urban area) what are the trade flows and prices which equilibrate commodity supplies and demands at each point? To define this problem more precisely, let π_i denote the commodity price at point i and let $D_i(\bar{\pi})$ and $S_i(\bar{\pi})$ denote the commodity demands and supplies at i as a function of the prices at all the points. Also let R_{ij} denote a set of shipment paths between i and j and let h_p be the commodity flow on path p. Then, a spatial price equilibrium may be defined as,

$$h_p[C_{ijp} + \pi_i - \pi_j] = 0, \qquad \forall(i, j, p \in R_{ij}),$$

$$C_{ijp} + \pi_i - \pi_j \geqq 0, \qquad \forall(i, j, p \in R_{ij}),$$

$$D_i(\bar{\pi}) - S_i(\bar{\pi}) + \sum_k \sum_{p \in R_{ik}} h_p - \sum_k \sum_{p \in R_{ki}} h_p = 0, \qquad \forall i,$$

$$\bar{h} \geqq 0, \qquad \bar{\pi} \geqq 0,$$

where C_{ijp} is the given cost of shipping a unit commodity on path $p \in R_{ij}$. The first two sets of equations are similar to Wardrop's [172] principle for network equilibrium. They say simply that for paths which are utilized, the delivered commodity price equals the destination commodity price and that for paths which are not used, the delivered price exceeds the destination price. The third set of equations simply state that the excess demand for each commodity at each point, taking trade into account, is zero. We solve the problem for the path flows $(\bar{h})$ and the local prices $(\bar{\pi})$ which must be nonnegative.

Takayama and Judge [167] showed how the above problem can be extended to intertemporal spatial excess demand systems. The shipment of a commodity through time allows representation of storage activities.

The spatial price equilibrium problem has a sound place in the interregional theory of trade. As such it awaits incorporation into general equilibrium models of the spatial economy. However, the somewhat less glorious fate of this problem to date has been to become synthesized with the model of traffic congestion on networks. This has occurred because of the strong mathematical similarity between the two problems rather than the substantive importance of congestion in trade flows. It has been simply assumed that path costs C_{ijp} are increasing functions of trade flows such that $C_{ijp} = C_p(h_p)$ where $p \in R_{ij}$. Paths are then defined on arc–node networks such that $\delta_{ap} = 1$ if arc a is on path p and $\delta_{ap} = 0$ otherwise. The above equations are now modified by substituting in the path cost functions and by defining trade flows on arcs such that,

$$f_a - \sum_p \delta_{ap} h_p = 0, \quad \forall a.$$

This last equation is nothing but a copy of the similar condition in the network congestion problem of Beckmann et al. [31] and brings with it all the same ambiguities which were critiqued earlier in this subsection. Attention then is focused on the mathematical properties of the model and the solution algorithms needed. For a representative article see Firesz et al. [58].

To date there has been no serious empirical validation of these models or careful reformulation of them. Regrettably, no careful distinction has been drawn between intraurban versus interregional spatial price equilibrium models. In the urban context, the flow of freight by trucks on urban roads is subject to exogenous congestion caused primarily by car traffic. In the interregional case significant congestion does not occur on network links (where again it is subject to exogenous traffic) but on freight terminals with fixed capacities for loading and unloading operations. These features are not incorporated into the literature. Combining the network problem of Beckmann et al. [31] with the spatial price equilibrium problem of Sammuelson [145] has proven to be an irresistible mathematical temptation. The resulting formulations await a context in reality.

3.2. The network design problem

The problem of network design represents the supply side in transportation planning but has received very little attention in this respect. The context of this problem is as follows. Suppose that there is a network of links and nodes denoted by N and that the problem is to select a network N' which consists of a subset of the links of N. The problem is to find the N' which minimizes total travel cost, is consistent with traffic equilibrium on it, given the traffic demands and is feasible to build for a given budget constraint. More precisely,

$$\underset{\{N' \in N\}}{\text{minimize}} \sum_{l \in N} f_l g_l(f_l)$$

subject to:

$$\sum_{l \in N'} k_l \le B$$

and,

$$f_l \in E(N').$$

Here, B is the budget level, k_l is the construction cost of network link l and $E(N')$ are the traffic network equilibrium conditions given by a minimization problem involving fixed or variable demands and deterministic or stochastic route choices. The outer minimization problem involves zero–one integer variables which denote inclusion in or exclusion from N', of the links in N.

Early attempts to formulate network design problems are due to Marble and Garrison [118] and Quandt [139] who used formulations based on the transportation problem of linear programming. Beckmann [27] and Werner [174] examined a more difficult problem in which only a set of nodes is given and the network configuration is to be solved for. Stairs [158], Ridley [144], Scott [148] and Boyce, Farhi and Weischedel [35] dealt with the problem of integer programming selection of links but ignored congestion. The last authors solved such problems heuristically for a network of 10 nodes and 45 links which were much harder than Scott's [148] 7 node, 21 link problems. Other heuristic approaches are due to Los [114] and Dionne and Florian [45].

An algorithm for solving the general problem presented above was formulated by Le Blanc [107] and applied by Boyce and Janson [36] for a small network. An extended problem is to write the link cost functions as $g_l(f_l, h_l)$ where h_l is the capacity (or width) of link l and to make link construction costs functions of capacity also: $k_l(h_l)$. Then, the capacities become decision variables in the network design problem. This formulation introduces a nonconvexity and makes solution much more difficult. Various attempts are by Dafermos [38], Dantzig, *et al.* [41] and Abdulaal and LeBlanc [1], and more recently by LeBlanc and Boyce [108].

3.3. The Herbert–Stevens linear programming model of land use allocation

Published in 1960, the linear programming model of Herbert and Stevens [83] was the first attempt to operationalize Alonso's theory of land use [2] to a general zonal representation of an urban area by assigning each land parcel to the highest bidding land use. Although the authors presented the model for the case of residential location it can be generalized to any number of land uses as long as the bid rent of each land use for each parcel is independent of the location decisions of other land uses.

The urban area is divided into $i = 1 \ldots I$ zones of land, of area L_i each. The population of households is classified into $h = 1 \ldots H$ internally homogeneous household classes of N^h households each. There are $k = 1 \ldots K$ dwelling types, each requiring q_k amount of land and construction cost C_{ik} per dwelling unit in zone i. We let X_{ik}^h be the number of type h households assigned to type k dwellings in zone i. Assuming that the number of households in each class is large relative to the combination of dwelling types and zones, we ignore the integer nature of households. In the original formulation of the model each land use, h has a predetermined fixed bid rent R_{ik}^h for each (i, k). Then the primal linear program is stated as,

$$\underset{\{X_{ik}^h\}}{\text{maximize}} \sum_h \sum_i \sum_k (R_{ik}^h - C_{ik}) X_{ik}^h$$

subject to:

$$\sum_h \sum_k q_k X_{ik}^h \leq L_i; \quad \text{each } i,$$

$$\sum_i \sum_k X_{ik}^h = N^h; \quad \text{each } h,$$

$$X_{ik}^h \geq 0 \quad \text{for all} \quad (i, k, h).$$

The objective function is the total profit from development to be maximized subject to constraints that the finite amount of land in each zone cannot be exceeded and that each household be located in some dwelling, somewhere. The dual of this linear program is:

$$\underset{\{V_i\},\{S^h\}}{\text{minimize}} \sum_i V_i L_i + \sum_h S^h N^h$$

subject to:

$$q_k V_i + S^h \geq R_{ik}^h - C_{ik}; \quad \text{each } (i, k, h),$$

$$V_i \geq 0 \quad \text{for each} \quad i.$$

Here V_i is the shadow price of land in zone i and S^h is the shadow price (or opportunity cost) of a type h household. Thus, the dual minimizes total resource costs with the qualification that S^h can be positive, zero or negative (representing an opportunity gain or benfit if negative), since it corresponds to an equality constraint in the primal.

If we drop the population constraints from the primal (and thus drop the S^h variables from the dual) we have the "open city" version of the Herbert–Stevens model: all the land will be developed and the numbers of each household type located will be endogenously determined. It is also possible to convert the land constraints to equalities by defining additional primal variables Y_i to be the amount of land in zone i kept in an alternative land use such as agriculture with a given bid rent R_i per unit of land. We then add Y_i to each ith land constraint writing it as an equality and we add $\sum_i R_i Y_i$ to the objective function.

Starting with the "open city" version, it is easy to see that the linear program represents a market equilibrium. Form complementary slackness theory we have the result that if $q_k V_i^* > R_{ik}^h - C_{ik}$ then $X_{ik}^{h*} = 0$, whereas if $q_k V_i^* = R_{ik}^h - C_{ik}$ then $X_{ik}^{h*} \geq 0$: a land use k will not occur in situation (i, k) unless profits from it can match the shadow price of the land it consumes. Also, if $Y_i > 0$ then $V_i^* = R_i$, namely if land is in excess supply for residential use it will be priced at its alternative use. It follows from these results that if two land uses, say h and m, can occur together in zone i they can only do so if they yield the same profit per unit of land, namely: $[R_{ik}^h - C_{ik}]/q_k = [R_{in}^m - C_{in}]/q_n = V_i^*$ where k and n are two dwelling types. Lower bidders per unit of land in i are excluded from i, and each land use is the highest or tied highest bidder wherever it is located.

In the closed version where the population constraints *are* imposed, the dual variable, S^h, is a subsidy to the locating land use h if it is negative and a tax on the land use h if it is positive. Since such a tax or subsidy does not exist in real markets, a value of S^h which differs from zero is an indication that households of type h need to raise their utility levels and thus bid lower if S^h is positive, or that they need to lower their utility levels and bid higher if S^h is negative. Underlying this idea is the definition of a bid rent function, $R_{ik}^h = f_{ik}^h(\bar{U}^h)$, as declining function of the utility level for households of the same preferences and income, namely the same type h.

It has been suggested by Wheaton [177] that the utility levels, $\bar{U}^h$ should play the role of the tax-subsidy variables, S^h. He proposed an iterative solution of the primal problem, using the magnitude and sign of the tax-subsidy variables to determine the adjustment in the utility levels. Since the dependence of bid rents on utility levels can be highly nonlinear there is no obvious convergence proof that all of the tax-subsidy terms can be eliminated by adjusting utility levels until all households of each type find location somewhere. Wheaton's conjecture that this can occur hinges crucially on assuming that lot-sizes, q_k, are continuous. This can be approximated by introducing a very dense but still discrete "continuum" of dwelling lot-sizes. If this is done, an equilibrium will occur such that $X_{ik}^{h*} \geq 0$ if $q_k V_i^* = f_{ik}^h(\bar{U}^{h*}) - C_{ik}$ and all households will be located somewhere. Although Wheaton's conjecture appears convincing, he provided no proof that it is indeed true, nor a proof that the iterative procedure is convergent.

There has been little interest since then in the further development of the Herbert–Stevens model or in its empirical application. This has been the case despite some truly promising empirical work earlier, by Britton Harris at the University of Pennsylvania. One effort is described in the unpublished report by Harris *et al.* [73] who used a linear programming algorithm inspired by the Herbert–Stevens model to evaluate various sketch plans based on the transport network for the proposed new town of Flummox, England: the linear program generated different land use configurations *given* different transport network configurations. Bid rent functions which incorporated the effect of travel cost were estimated from households in Hartford, Connecticut who were presumed to have preferences similar to those who would have resided in Flummox. Harris also proposed linear programming for sketch plan analysis in the Penn–Jersey Transportation Study. Harris' algorithm included the idea of utility level adjustments and this work provided the basis for Wheaton's later but clearer treatment of the subject. It is unfortunate that the above empirical study is rather poorly documented and thus does not provide reliable evidence of the model's performance in the urban planning context.

There are two other noteworthy adaptations of the Herbert–Stevens model. One has been discussed in Anas [4; Ch. 1] where it is proposed that the model can be used to allocate households to existing dwellings as well as to newly built ones. Such a formulation determines vacancies in places where not all of the existing stock is occupied and yields a dual variable corresponding to a short run equilibrium quasi-rent of zero. Vacancies occur in places where no household's bid per dwelling less operating costs incurred by the landlord are positive.

Another adaptation proposed by Ben Shahar, Mazor and Pines [33] is to use the model to plan land development over time. To do so we need to imagine a few small changes in the model's notation. Instead of dwelling types, we define land use sequences. For example, a sequence may be: vacant land for a number of years, followed by single family homes followed by multifamily dwellings. Land use per dwelling may now be denoted as q_{kt} for the tth year in the sequence, k. The bid price of a sequence is the present values of its yearly bid rents less yearly costs less periodic construction and adjustment costs. A decision to implement a sequence automatically implies future land consumption levels and dwelling type availabilities for each year. We can then set up constraints which allocate the population of each year to the dwelling stock of that year, assuming population relocates without cost, and constraints which assure that the land in each zone is not exceeded in any one year. Such a formulation is a discrete analogue to the continuous formulations which Fujita [59] has examined later using the techniques of control theory in a monocentric land use context. Obviously, the linear program would allocate land at the early years to sequences which increase in dwelling density over time if population levels increase over time. This approach would confirm the, by now well understood, results that during regimes of population growth it may be efficient to build in the preriphery first reserving more strategically located land for later and more dense development. The approach would also confirm the result established by Fujita [59]: land uses and highly dissimilar time profiles will occur in the same locations as long as their present value profit per unit of land for their sequence is the same making them equal present value bidders. Using a conjecture similar to Wheaton's, the tax-subsidy terms which are now attached to each land use in each year can be driven to zero by appropriate adjustment of each land use's utility level in each year.

While the above adaptations of the original Herbert–Stevens algorithm seek more general results, there has been a recent effort by Anderson [14] to reexamine the model under stronger assumptions or for narrower problems in order to gain a higher level of tractability. Anderson demonstrated that when all dwelling units are identical except for location (i.e. there is only one dwelling type) then there is a version of the Herbert–Stevens model which produces a market equilibrium. To obtain this version it is necessary to replace the coefficients which are bid rents for dwellings with the difference between the bid rent for a dwelling and the bid rent for an arbitrarily selected reference dwelling. Then these differences are constant for each household and do not vary with the level of utility. The level of utility itself is directly implied by the tax-subsidy term for each household. Furthermore, the problem reduces to a "pure transportation problem in linear programming" so that the coefficients which are bid rent differences can be replaced with differences between the transportation cost of a household at a certain location and the transportation cost of the household at its reference location. As we shall see in the next section of this article, such transportation problems have been used as market clearing algorithms in both the Urban Institute and National Bureau of Economic Research Models.

3.4. Mills' linear programming model and extensions

A shortcoming of the Herbert–Stevens approach is that it does not provide a framework for examining the interactions among the different sectors of the urban economy. Such interactions are presumably reflected in the exogenously given bid rent functions. At the same time, the solution of the model is a land use allocation that could give rise to revised bid rents. If, for example, we were to use this model to allocate workplaces and residences with given bid rent functions, we would find that residential bid rents must be recomputed to reflect proximity to employment locations obtained in the initial solution.

Mills' linear programming model [124, 126] published in 1972 provides an elegant and simple solution to the simultaneous allocation of several land uses: production, housing and transportation. The crux of Mills' model is a Leontieff-type constant coefficient technology. The urban area produces predetermined (target) quantities of a number of export commodities by means of various activities which employ different ratios of land, labor and capital and correspond to production in buildings of different heights. In Mills' original formulation housing is the only locally consumed commodity. The other commodities are all exported through a central port or terminal. The urban area is represented as a square grid system with a similarly oriented road network. A key feature of Mills' model is that all traffic and the resulting congestion is accounted for and the amount of land allocated to roads is determined endogeneously throughout the urban area. This becomes possible by approximating the nonlinar congestion functions as piecewise linear step functions.

The optimizing principle employed by Mills is to minimize the total cost of the urban area (including transport congestion) under the assumption that land is bought at the agricultural land price and capital and labor are imported at given national prices. The size and internal structure of the urban area are determined by the production targets for the export goods and the production activity technology which is available. The dual linear program produces appropriate shadow prices which allow an efficient market interpretation of the allocation save for the externality of congestion. Mills shows the model can be used to determine the optimal congestion toll structure so that the externality is internalized. The linear and cost oriented nature of the model, however, means that the market behavior of households is one of cost minimization rather than the maximization of a nonlinear utility function. Nevertheless, Mills' model is the most direct and only successful attempt to operationalize the monocentric urban economic theory. The linear program produces the concentration of production around the center with a sharply declining building height and density gradient, and housing located around the production activity.

In another paper, Mills [126] demonstrated how the existence of several predetermined export nodes can be introduced to create a multinucleated urban form. Hartwick and Hartwick [76] extended Mills' original model by including intermediate goods in the production of the export commodities. This is done by allowing the different industries to interact by means of a physical input–output technology, so that other commodities as well as land, capital and labor are used in the production of each export commodity. In such a model it is the relative locations of the various production activities that is of interest. Various configurations are possible depending on the relative cost of transporting the different commodities and the cost of personal commuting which determines the distribution of housing. In another extension, Kim [98] used the model to derive the result that as cities get larger and the intensity of land use in the center increases, it becomes efficient to build transit systems and subways near the center. More recently, Moore [130] developed a dynamic perfect foresight equilibrium version of Mills' model replacing the fixed production targets with endogeneously determined production at fixed exogenous export prices. The model also takes into account the redevelopment of land with adjustment costs that increase with land use density. Simulations show the sprawl and discontinuous nature of land development in a perfect foresight context.

Despite its great flexibility and the appealing general equilibrium structure, there have been no empirical applications of this linear programming approach to date. One reason is the difficulty of describing an urban area by means of a grid or other regular geometry which is necessary for the tractability of the model. Another reason is the computational limits which are reached when such linear programs increase in dimensionality. There is also the lack of appropriate fixed coefficient data for describing the industrial aggregates to be included in the model. Finally, there is the fact that linear programs produce sharply defined boundaries among land uses, whereas various heterogeneities should cause similar land uses to locate in a mixed pattern. This last feature, as we saw, is dealt better by discrete choice models (see Anas [4], Anas and Cho [8]).

3.5. The Koopmans–Beckmann quadratic assignment problem

In 1957 Koopmans and Beckmann published their still celebrated article in which they claimed to have posed a problem central to location theory. Suppose there are $k = 1 \ldots N$ indivisible facilities such as plants, dams in a river valley etc. and an *equal* number of sites. They went further and assumed that each site can accommodate only one facility and that each facility needed only one site. Then, they asked: is the assignment of facilities to sites which maximizes total net revenues (or profit) sustainable by a set of market rents? This is an example of the general problem in economics: the correspondence of a market equilibrium to a Pareto optimum. In this particular problem the complication arises from the fact that the facilities are interdependent by means of flows between them which incur transportation costs. In the authors' example plants were connected together by the flow of intermediate commodities from one plant to another. The size of each plant or facility is predetermined by increasing returns to scale or agglomerative economies. An interesting application of this problem may be to think of each facility as an activity complex: an agglomeration of different land uses such as an urban subcenter. Then the problem becomes one of optimal urban form with multiple subcenters. Much is lost, however, by the assumption that the number of sites must equal the number of facilities. This, as we shall see is a central limitation in the Koopmans–Beckmann problem [105].

If we let a_{ki} be the nonnegative profit of plant k in location i and P_{ki} be the 0, 1 permutation matrix such that $P_{ki} = 1$ if k is assigned to i and $P_{ki} = 0$ if k is not assigned to i then the total profit to be maximized is

$$\pi = \sum_{k,i} a_{ki} P_{ki}.$$

Without interactions among plants this is a complete statement and the authors went on to prove that there are always market sustainable optimal assignments such that unique site rents can be computed to decentralize the optimal assignment. Their proof hinges on reformulating the problem as a linear assignment problem subject to constraints which enforce the integer nature of the assignments. Thus, let $X_{ki} = 1$ if k is assigned to i and $X_{ki} = 0$ otherwise. Then (without imposing these integer restrictions) we

$$\underset{\{X_{ki}\}}{\text{maximize}} \sum_{k,i} a_{ki} X_{ki}$$

subject to:

$$\sum_i X_{ki} \leq 1, \qquad k = 1, \ldots, N;$$

$$\sum_k X_{ki} \leq 1, \qquad i = 1, \ldots, N;$$

each

$$X_{ki} \geq 0.$$

From duality theory, if we renumber so that plant k is optimally matched with site k, we can show the result that for any other site i,

$$a_{kk} - a_{ki} \leq \gamma_k - \gamma_i$$

where γ_k, γ_i are the site rents. This condition states that each site goes to the highest bidding plant or that differential site rents are the envelope of differential profits. This linear form of the Koopmans–Beckmann problem is free of the price-sustainability difficulties that arise in the quadratic case to be discussed below. In the linear case the optimal assignment is market sustainable. While the linear version of the model is not as famous as the quadratic one it has been used to cultivate theoretical insight. For example, Lind [111] has employed the linear assignment model to study the connection between property values and air pollution abatement benefits, showing that differential property values between sites correctly reflect the benefits of clean air in situations where households are limited to a discrete number of locations in space. Similarly, Wildasin [183] uses the linear assignment model to show that property values reflect the benefits of local public goods when the number of local communities (suppliers of public goods) chosen by households is arbitrary but finite. Such uses of the Koopmans–Beckmann model are interesting but of limited scope because the propositions established by Lind [111] and Wildasin [183] are known to hold under the more general conditions of continuous locational adjustments.

In the problem with interplant commodity flows, the authors assumed that a fixed quantity b_{kl} flowed from plant k to l independent of the location of these plants. Also each unit of any flow was transported at cost c_{ij} from i to j, subject to the triangle inequality $c_{ij} \leq c_{ik} + c_{kj}$, for $i, j, k = 1 \ldots N$.

In this case the net revenue (or profit) to be maximized is

$$\pi = \sum_{k,i} a_{ki} P_{ki} - \sum_{k,l} \sum_{i,j} b_{kl} P_{ki} c_{ij} P_{lj}.$$

The equivalent linear assignment problem which results in integer solutions is,

$$\underset{\{X_{ki}\}, \{X_{kl,ij}\}}{\text{maximize}} \sum_{k,i} a_{ki} X_{ki} - \sum_{k,l} \sum_{i,j} c_{ij} X_{kl,ij}$$

$$X_{ki} b_{kl} + \sum_j X_{kl,ji} = X_{li} b_{kl} + \sum_j X_{kl,ij}$$

$$\sum_i X_{ki} = 1, \qquad k = 1, \ldots, N$$

$$\sum_k X_{ki} = 1, \qquad i = 1, \ldots, N$$

$$X_{ki} \geq 0, \qquad X_{kl,ij} \geq 0, \qquad X_{kl,ii} = 0.$$

The first constraint states that the production of the intermediate commodity (k,l) at site i plus the inflow of (k, l) to i as measured by the second summation on the left must equal the total consumption (or demand for) (k, l) at i plus the outflow of (k, l) from i. The solution has the property that if k locates at i and l locates at j then $X_{kl,ij} = b_{kl}$ but zero otherwise.

The authors examined market sustainability under the assumption that site profits are uniform, i.e. $a_{ki} = a_k$ and thus reduced the problem to one of transport cost minimization. They showed that in this case an assignment is not price sustainable but claimed this result to be much more general. Hartwick [75] proposed a counter-example which was shown later to be wrong by Heffley [78] who did provide valid examples of sustainable optimal assignments under the assumption that profits, a_{ki}, can vary over sites. He also derived a necessary condition for sustainability. Heffley [79] also proved the nonexistence of an equilibrium solution to the original Koopmans–Beckmann formulation by demonstrating that the underlying market game was empty.

The problem of market failure in the integer assignment problem is not too dissimilar from the market failure problem in the Herbert and Stevens [83] model discussed in 3.3. In both models bid rents (or profits which are in fact bid rents) are fixed. Hamilton [69] has argued that the a_{ki} should be increasing functions of the number of plants to locate in a site (why should a site take only one plant?). Similarly, two plants located in close proximity should have higher commodity flows between them in order to take advantage of lower transport costs. Such modifications make the problem continuous and allow us to explicitly consider agglomeration and site congestion as externalities. Then, appropriate taxes imposed on these externalities should allow a market sustainable solution. Indeed, Hartwick and Hartwick's [76] extension of Mills' [124] linear programming model deals with interplant commodity shipments and produces agglomerations of different firms. In retrospect, then, the Koopmans–Beckmann problem appears not to have been very useful as a model relevant to urban economics. In this field it has been surpassed. However, it still retains much appeal in operation research circles where the integer assignment of indivisible resources to sites (or positions) is of considerable interest. In such contexts, however, market sustainability is not an issue.

Interesting attempts to build normative models of urban form and land use design based on the Koopmans–Beckmann problem were originated by Los [113] and Hopkins [86]. Los combined the Koopmans–Beckmann problem with the network design problem (see Section 3.2). Given a network of nodes and links, which indivisible facilities should be assigned to which nodes and which links of the network should be built so that total facility and network construction costs are minimized and interfacility shipments are accomodated on the network? Los's contribution was to show the combinatorial complexity of this problem and to demonstrate that fast heuristic algorithms can obtain good solutions for fairly small problems of about 10 or so facilities. Computational cost, in such problems, grows very quickly with the number of facilities.

Such integer models of urban form are now quite crude compared

to the sophistication and flexibility of economic models. Furthermore, the lack of market substainability makes them unappealing to
economists but perhaps less so to town planners and operations
researchers who often operate from a different perspective.
Nevertheless, urban economists have yet to develop mathematical
programming models in which agglomeration economies, scale
economies and indivisible public facilities are properly included.

4. ECONOMETRIC MODELS

The models discussed in this part have features in common with the
non-economic empirically oriented models of Part 2, and with the
monocentric simulation models of part 1. With the former they
share a committment to actual data from which model equations are
to be estimated. With the latter they share a committment to
microeconomics from which model equations are theoretically
derived. At the same time, these econometric models go beyond the
other model groups in a number of ways. First, there is the use of
econometric techniques to estimate the models' equations. As a
result the availability of data and its aggregation play an important
role in determining the models' specification. Second, these models
have been developed in response to certain urban policy problems
and they are used to evaluate appropriate government programs or
planning options. Third, these models are not concerned with
optimization (as were the models of Part 3) but with market
forecasting exclusively. Fourth, the solution of the models on the
computer, in most cases, requires complex numerical procedures.
Fifth, in all cases the models' development undergoes a number of
successive major refinements and improvements incorporating attempts to deal with limitations encountered in previous phases of
the models' development.
    If there is a final feature that ought to be noted, it is that the
housing market is the central concern in all of these models which
have been implemented. Indeed, it would not have been inappropriate to have grouped them under the title of "econometric
models of the housing market." Nevertheless, with the possible
exception of the Urban Institute Model, the creators of these
models have anticipated their expansion to include non-housing

sectors and in some cases, they have indeed undertaken such expansion.

Unlike the other model groups, the econometric models have been developed in the seventies and eighties, after urban economic theory had a major impact on the thinking of urban economists. Around this time it became apparent that urban economic theory provided a wealth of ideas whereby government policies and programs can be subjected to the scrutiny of cost-benefit analysis and the econometric models emerged as a response to this challenge.

In discussing these models we need to focus on the following aspects. First, we need to address the extent to which the models conform to the theory, the points of departure from the theory and the reasons why such departure may or may not be justified. Second, we need to address the empirical estimation of the models, in other words the econometric techniques which have been used and the rigor with which data has been treated. Third, we need to evaluate the policy application of the models in order to determine whether they have yielded significant quantitative findings. The emphasis on quantitative rather than qualitative findings is especially relevant for these models since qualitative answers are, for the most part, obtainable from monocentric simulation models. Why then the expense to develop and test econometric models? Presumably, the reason for undertaking these efforts is to be able to quantitatively analyze the market effects of actual government policies, projects and programs. To put it bluntly, these models may be viewed as having failed if they have not yielded reliable quantitative findings about the problems to which they have been applied. Unfortunately, the question of whether a particular model has succeeded in this way or not is largely a matter of judgement. Usually, not enough published information about the results of estimation and policy application is available to be able to decide the issue with confidence.

4.1. The Urban Institute Model for housing market analysis

The earliest form of the Urban Institute Model was published by deLeeuw and Struyk [42] in 1975. Their model contained four actors: (a) households (the consumers of housing), (b) existing dwellings and their owners or landlords, (c) builders of new dwellings and (d) the government. Households chose the utility maximizing quantity of housing in new or existing dwellings and among a number of zones. Landlords determined a supply function offering various price–quality combinations of housing. Builders supplied new housing at a horizontal supply curve, offering the demanded quantity at the cost it takes to supply one unit of housing quantity. The government was envisioned to influence the housing market via a number of instruments such as tax charges, housing allowances, minimum new construction requirements and minimum quantitites of housing services per dwelling (or housing standards).

The most unusual feature of the model is the way in which households and dwellings are aggregated into types. This is done in such a way that first the number of household types equals the number of dwelling types. This is a peculiar departure from theory. As we saw, in the monocentric simulation literature there was no need to impose a requirement that the number of rings or zones into which the land market is divided be equal to the number of land uses seeking location in this market. Secondly, it is assumed, in the Urban Institute Model, that the number of households in each type is the same as the number of dwellings in each type. For example, an urban area with 300,000 households and thus 300,000 occupied dwellings could be disaggregated into 30 households and an equal number of dwelling types each consisting of 10,000 households or dwellings. These assumptions allow the model to match a household type with one dwelling type just as in the Koopmans–Beckmann [105] problem plants are matched to sites. If a household type is allocated to new dwellings, this requires construction of 10,000 new dwellings and removal from the market of 10,000 existing dwellings (that dwelling type which remains unoccupied). In no other model of the housing market are similar assumptions utilized. In the Herbert–Stevens [83] model, for example, there can be unequal numbers of household and dwelling types and each type can have an arbitrary number of households or dwellings. The apparent reason for this assumption in the Urban Institute Model is that it greatly facilitates computations in the search for a solution. What is not clear in the various documenta- tions of the model is the violence that this definition of household and dwelling types does to the data and the empirical realism of the results. The drawbacks from these definitions can be minimized by considering a very large number of households and dwellings. Indeed, the procedure is strictly correct only at the limit when each household and each dwelling are treated as a separate "type." This however, is impractical and far from the reality of the model which operates with a small number of household and dwelling types, thus introducing a substantial artificial indivisibility which has no counterpart in reality. Although I believe these assumptions could seriously influence the quantitative conclusions of the model, I am not prepared to argue that the qualitative results would be seriously changed.

We now turn to a discussion of the model's mathematical relationships. The utility of the jth dwelling to the ith household is measured by,

$$U_{ij} = H_{ij} X_{ij} Z_{1ij} Z_{2j} Z_{3ij}$$

where, H_{ij} measures "effective housing services (above a subsistence level) enjoyed by the ith household type from the jth dwelling type," X_{ij} measures other goods and services and Z_1 through Z_3 measure characteristics of the geographic zone where the jth dwelling is located. Note that i and j hereafter refer to the entire stock of ith and jth type households and dwellings.

The five terms in the utility function are defined as follows:

$$H_{ij} = [Q_j - \gamma_1 \alpha_i Y_i/P_n]^{\alpha_i}, \qquad 0 < \alpha_i < 1,$$

$$X_{ij} = [(Y_i - Q_j P_j) - \gamma_1(1 - \alpha_i)Y_i]^{1-\alpha_i},$$

$$Z_{1ij} = (200 - T_j)^{0.5 + \alpha_i - \alpha_1},$$

$$Z_{2j} = \left[\frac{\overline{P_j - P_o}}{\underline{P_j - P_o}} \right]^{0.01\gamma_2},$$

$$Z_{3ij} = R_{ij} + (1000/(100\gamma_3 + 1)).$$

In the above, Q_j is the "quantity of housing services" offered by dwelling j and the quantity $\gamma_1 \alpha_i Y_i/P_n$ is a minimum acceptable housing quantity for household i given that household's model income, Y_i, and the unit price of new housing services P_n.

The first neighborhood characteristic Z_1, measures the utility of the monthly hours of leisure, $200 - T_j$, available after T_j monthly hours of commuting are incurred by the average commuter (worker) residing in zone j with the coefficient α_1 the value of α_i for "white nonelderly families." Z_1 incorporates a stylized fact assumption that households value travel time at about $1/2$ their hourly wage. The second zone characteristic, Z_2, is intended to measure relative zonal wealth as the ratio of $\overline{P_j} - P_o$ (the average net rent of a zone which is gross rent less operating costs, P_o being the minimum operating costs per unit of housing services), to $\overline{\overline{P_j - P_o}}$, the average net rent in the metropolitan area, with $\gamma_2 > 0$ measuring a positive preference for wealthy zones. The third characteristic, Z_3, measures racial preferences. R_{ij} is the proportion of households in the zone of dwelling j belonging to the same racial group as household i and $\gamma_3 > 0$ expresses the strength of preference for racial homogeneity. This form of Z_3 implies symmetrical preferences across racial groups with whites and blacks having the same attitude toward homogeneity. The treatment of "zonal wealth" and "racial preferences" is an ambitious attempt by the designers of the model to capture important residential externalities, a feature which is absent from other econometric simulation models.

We note also from the demand function that it implies an income elasticity for housing services, H_{ij}, equal to $+1$ and a price elasticity for housing services equal to -1. Note, however, that elasticities with respect to the *quantity* of housing services, Q_j, are not unitary because the utility function is of the Stone–Geary type with income and price dependent levels of subsistence consumption. Evidence more recent than the Urban Institute Model suggest that the price elasticity may be around -0.5 (see Mayo [119] for a survey).

The minimum acceptable (or subsistence) level of housing services increases with income and decreases with the unit price, γ_1 being an empirical parameter measuring "the degree to which households will alter their housing choice in response to a price discount" and α_i is a parameter expressing the strength of housing preferences versus other goods for the ith household. Similarly, $\gamma_1(1 - \alpha_i) Y_i$ is the minimum quantity of other goods. Note that with $0 \leq \gamma_1 \leq 1$, when $\gamma_1 = 0$ utility becomes Cobb–Doublas whereas when $\gamma_1 = 1$ no choice is allowed to the household.

On the supply side, the owners of existing dwellings maximize expected discounted profits subject to a production function for housing services. The profit function is,

$$\pi = P_j Q_j - P_o Q_j - P_c X_j - F_j$$

where P_o is operating cost per unit of housing service, P_j is the market price per unit of service and P_c is new capital costs per unit of capital inputs and X_j is additional capital inputs into the existing unit, with F_j the fixed costs due to previously purchased capital. The production function is:

$$Q_j = \left[\beta_1 + \left(2\beta_2 \frac{X_j}{Q_o} \right)^{0.5} \right] Q_o$$

where Q_o is the level of housing services provided by the dwelling one period earlier. Thus adding capital into an existing structure has a positive but declining marginal productivity, and with no additional capital inputs ($X_j = 0$), an existing unit depreciates at a rate $1 - \beta_1$.

Expected discounted profits are expressed as

$$\pi^e = \left(\frac{1+r}{1+r-\beta_1\lambda} \right)(P_j - P_o)Q_j - \left(\frac{1+r}{r} \right)(P_c X_j + F_j)$$

where r is the rate of discount and λ is the rate at which rent less operating cost is expected to decline over time. Then, maximization of π^e subject to the production function and with respect to X_j yields,

$$Q_j = \left[\beta_1 + \left(\frac{2}{3} \right)\beta_2 \left(\frac{P_j - P_o}{P_c} \right) \right] Q_o$$

where the assumption $r/(r + 1 - \beta_1\lambda) = \frac{2}{3}$ is imposed.

Next one can derive the household's bid rent curve (an indifference curve between P_j and Q_j) which has the shape shown in Figure 4. From this diagram we see that Q_m, the minimum quantity standard, and P_o and P_n are key exogenous variables together with incomes Y_i and travel times T_j. The model's endogenous output includes prices and quantities for each existing and new dwelling, number of new dwellings and removals, assignment of households to dwellings and zonal averages of prices, quantities, incomes and racial proportions.

Other features of the model are the following: (a) It deals with decade long changes in the housing market without tracing annual changes during the decade. Thus, for example, the quantity Q_o represents the quantity of housing at the beginning of the decade. (b) The metropolitan area is generally divided into five zones some

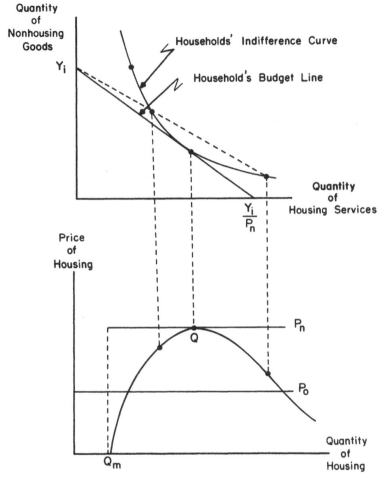

FIGURE 4   Prices and quantities in the Urban Institute Model.

representing the city and others the suburbs. Existing dwelling types can occur in these zones while all new construction is assumed to occur in a non-geographic zone. (c) Household types are collected into white non-elderly families, white elderly and/or single person households, black non-elderly families and black elderly and/or single person households. (d) The model relies on an objective housing quantity concept, same for all households. This requires observing total payments for housing and then dividing by the price per unit quantity, P_j, to obtain the quantity of housing, Q_j. (e) Furthermore, the above procedure is done by combining renters with homeowners and pretending, in essence, that owners rent from themselves. The original publication of the Urban Institute Model did include a modified model in which households were allowed tenure choice (to own or to rent). (f) Finally, an advantage of this model is that it can be readily applied to any metropolitan area covered in the U.S. Census. In the original publication [42] the authors reported parallel applications of the model to Durham, N.C.; Austin, Texas; Portland, Oregon; Pittsburgh; Washington, D.C. and Chicago.

The solution procedure of the model seeks to establish a market equilibrium which conforms well with theory with the exception of several departures from it. These "equilibrium" conditions are: (a) that each household type be allocated to that dwelling type which yields the maximum utility among all available dwelling types including new construction; (b) that each existing dwelling be either occupied by a single household or be vacant at the minimum price; (c) that total profits over all existing dwellings be maximized given that (a) and (b) hold. These conditions would represent a "market equilibrium" in the absence of any racial externalities. Condition (c) is in fact claimed by the authors to be nearly always equivalent to one in which each dwelling maximizes profit. Since the model includes racial externalities it can presumably generate nonunique solutions satisfying the market equilibrium conditions (a)–(c). In order to choose one among such solutions, the authors postulate condition (d) which appears a plausible but ad-hoc criterion. This condition selects the market equilibrium pattern in which the racial distribution of households deviates the least from the initial racial distribution pattern.

The solution algorithm discussed by the authors (in [42]) assigns households to dwellings arbitrarily and performs computations of the equilibrium price-quantity bundles for each assignment. Then conditions (a)–(c) are checked and the assignment changed until these conditions are satisfied. Outer iterations are performed to see if the resulting racial patterns satisfy condition (d).

The model's estimation follows a rather simple logic. It should be evident by now that the model relies on a very small number of coefficients to be estimated. Furthermore, as we saw, many important coefficients such as price and income elasticities are fixed or strongly restricted a priori. The remaining coefficients are not estimated simultaneously but piece-meal using specially tailored statistical procedures for each coefficient. Finally, there are a number of adjustment procedures which are used by trial and error to improve the model's fit to the data given the estimated coefficient values. Some of these adjustment procedures change the data itself. For example, if estimated coefficients result in equilibrium rent predictions which are too low, the census reported vacancies may be decreased in the belief that some of these represent housing stock which is permanently abandoned. Clearly the sequential and highly selective calibration procedures of the Urban Institute Model cannot be claimed to result in any unique coefficient set, nor is it possible to claim that the estimated coefficients are such that the entire model's predictions are maximum likelihood. The creators of the model do not seem to be perturbed by such ambiguities in the model's empirical validation.

The model lends itself to rather straightforward analyses of key housing market policies. Chiefly, these are: (a) housing allowances to households consuming very low quantities of housing, (b) income redistribution without earmarking for housing, (c) construction subsidies, (d) changes in government minimum standards for new housing. Furthermore these policies can be analyzed for various urban environments such as rapid versus slow growth, high versus low percentage of minorities and elastic versus inelastic supply functions.

The most important policies, (a) housing allowances and (b) construction subsidies, are compared incisively in [43]. A housing allowance allocated to low income households consuming low level housing quantity raises housing prices in higher quantity levels. Over time, however, these price increases are dissipated as new construction responds, lowering the price of housing. Recipients of allowances benefit despite the higher prices. Under a construction subsidy low income groups benefit but after a longer time span as higher quantity housing filters down to them. The new construction subsidy may be the preferred policy (yields higher benefits in the same time span) when supply is inelastic. At the qualitative level these results are not surprising at all and could be deduced by an economist familiar with some stylized facts in the theory of housing demand and supply (see, for example, Mills [127]). Quantitative results on the other hand, are not stressed much in the published material perhaps because they are not considered reliable.

In another application [170] the model was used to predict the market effects of actual housing allowance programs in the 1970's in Green Bay, Wisconsin and in South Bend, Indiana. In Green Bay, where population growth has been rapid the model predicted small price increases due to the program, whereas in South Bend which is losing population and stock, participants in the program are predicted to have to pay relatively much higher prices to obtain improved housing.

More recently, the model has been applied to a more diverse set of policy issues. A paper by Struyk and Turner [160] examines the effects of racial preferences on the housing market. The authors synthesize a Northeastern and Western prototype city from census data and simulate their growth under two assumptions: (a) that whites care about the racial composition of their neighborhood and (b) that whites are neutral to racial composition. Blacks are assumed to be neutral to racial composition in both cases. Under the first scenario blacks are found to be more widely dispersed within the city in the West than in the Northeast. Under the second scenario whites turn to center city housing than to new construction, raising prices for black households located in the central cities and reducing their consumption. The model implies, therefore, that a reduction of prejudice would adversely affect blacks in the housing market.

Finally, a recent extensive application by Turner and Struyk [169] attempts to evaluate the course of the U.S. national housing market in the decade of the 1980's and to compare the effects of some Reagan administration policies on housing consumption in the decade. The answers are derived by introducing assumptions about broad economic forces, housing finance trends, government assisted housing programs, welfare policy and tax policy. The overall conclusion is that the quality of housing occupied by Americans would have improved over the 1980 to 1987 period irrespective of whether first term Reagan or second term Carter policies were in effect.

4.2. The National Bureau of Economic Research Model

This model (NBER, in brief) was initiated by research support from
the Department of Housing and Urban Development in 1968 and
has been a nearly continuously ongoing project since then. There
appear to be at least four successive versions of the model starting
with the Detroit prototype [88] and followed by Pittsburgh I,
Pittsburgh II and Chicago [92, 93]. The most recent version of the
model [94] has been rebaptized the Harvard Urban Development
Simulation Model (or HUDS). Like the Urban Institute Model, the
NBER model aims at being a model of the housing market with
appropriate demand and supply side representations. There, all
similarities between the two models come to an end.

The designers of the Urban Institute (UI) Model have shown a
strong preference for a highly portable, highly aggregated yet
behaviorally rich, small but realistic model strongly rooted in the
theory. For a number of reasons, the designers of the NBER model
preferred to design a very large scale (and not easily portable),
highly disaggregated model which makes a number of significant
departures from the theory. For example, while the UI model is an
equilibrium model operating over a decade, the NBER model is an
explicitly disequilibrium model operating over a sequence of years.
While the UI model focuses exclusively on the housing sector, the
NBER model's housing sector is linked to a number of subsidiary
submodels which "prepare the stage" for the clearing of the housing
market. On the demand side there are submodels for exogenous
and population serving employment, for demographic change, for
job changes, for the generation of movers in the housing market,
the generation of new households and finally the creation of housing
demand and tenure decisions. On the supply side, there are
submodels for land use, the formation of expectations, new
construction, and structure conversion. The UI model is highly
aggregated in dwelling, household and geographic categories whereas the NBER model seeks a high level of disaggregation in these
respects. For example, the Pittsburgh I version deals with 11
industries, 20 workplaces and 50 residence zones. Ten structure
types, 2 neighborhood types and 2 housing quality classes combine
into 40 housing types (or bundles) and there are 96 household types
crossclassified by 12 life cycle categories, 4 income brackets and 2

levels of education. If we consider that the 96 households can also be classified by the available industries and workplaces, then there are in fact $20 \times 11 \times 96 = 21,120$ possible "types" of households on the demand side to be allocated in the market. On the supply side there are 40 housing types by 50 residence zones or a potential of 2,000 dwelling submarkets. The problem of market clearing is then viewed as the allocation of these 21,120 household types to the 2,000 submarkets. Incidentially, the types of households and dwellings are not defined to have a one to one correspondance as in the UI model (a fact which should be obvious from the above discussion). Multiplying 21,120 by 2,000 there are precisely 42,240,000 cells in an allocation matrix representing possible assignments. This number is roughly 50 times or so the number of households in Pittsburgh! Of course, the designers of the model are aware that an overwhelming number of these matrix entries will have zero households assigned to them in the observed data. However, they can hardly give us reasonable assurance that the predicted nonzero assignments will correspond very closely with the observed nonzero entries. Yet, they appear to be convinced, and make a plausible case of it, that this level of detail is necessary to analyse the effects of certain policies such as housing allowances on various households types.

The size of the computational problem creates data storage and processing difficulties which force them in the direction of using list storage processing. In the Detroit prototype the model was aggregative. However, starting with Pittsburgh I, the designers wisely resorted to a microsimulation technique whereby samples of households and available dwellings were matched. For example in the Pittsburgh and Chicago simulations 72,000 and 84,000 occupied and unoccupied units are processed respectively once during each simulation period. After sequential processing by the demographic, job change, movers and new household formation submodels, a "demand list" consisting of 12,000 to 18,000 households is created. These are then sorted by workzone, income, life cycle and education. Next, the demand submodel performs an assignment of each household in the demand list of one of the 50 types of dwellings.

In the Detroit prototype which did not use microsimulation, households of a certain type were distributed among the dwelling type submarkets by means of linear demand functions, such that the number of households of a certain type choosing a dwelling type was a linear function of the "minimum gross price" of that dwelling type. This assignment could not guarantee that the assigned demand would not be larger than the total available demand, nor that the assigned demand would be positive. Furthermore, linear demand functions did nothing to capture the substitution of various bundles for each other. Starting with the Pittsburgh model [92], the designers replaced these linear demand functions with multinomial logit functions which resolved the problems mentioned.

These multinomial logit functions have the following form:

$$P_{hk} = \frac{S_k^{\alpha_h} e^{\beta_h \min_i(R_{ikh}) + \gamma_{kh}}}{\sum_{m=1}^{50} S_m^{\alpha_h} e^{\beta_h \min_i(R_{imh}) + \gamma_{mh}}},$$

where h denotes a household type of a certain income, race, life cycle position and workplace. S_m is the number of dellings of type m available in the entire market and R_{ikh} is the gross price (or rent) of a type k dwelling in geographic zone i for household type h. P_{hk}, then, is the probability that a household of type h will choose any dwelling of type k or, in effect, will choose the kth submarket. The coefficients α_h, β_h and γ_{kh} can be estimated econometrically and the designers report estimates of β_h (see [92]) but do not report standard errors. Of course, $\beta_h < 0$ and $\alpha_h > 0$ with γ_{kh}, a dummy coefficient unrestricted in sign. The reported estimates of β_h are a bit peculiar because they imply price elasticities of submarket demands ranging from -0.88 to -3.08 with most cases well over -1.00. Such elasticities are at great variance with nearly all studies of housing demand (see Mayo [119]) which confirm values of -0.5 or so. Lerman [110] and Anas [4], having estimated similar multinomial logit models of housing demand, reported (or implied) elasticities within the range of the literature surveyed by Mayo [119].

The precise econometric technique used to obtain the estimates is not reported by Kain and Apgar [93]. Standard maximum likelihood procedures developed by McFadden [121] would have enabled standard error computations.

An important issue in the NBER model is the computation of the gross price (or rent). What is assumed according to the authors is that dwellings of the same type in different locations are identical in attributes and that therefore households need only consider the lowest price location for the dwellings of the same type (thus, the use of the minimum gross rent across locations). A more precise statement of their assumption would be that dwellings of the same type are identical in their observed attributes and that the unobserved attributes of dwellings are correlated (assuming, $0 < \alpha_h < 1$) but not across locations. These assumptions (discussed by McFadden [122] and Anas [4]) are needed to argue that the choice probabilities are consistent with utility maximization. Another peculiarity with the multinomial logit model used by the authors is that only price enters the utility function. Other dwelling attributes such as room sizes, age, quality, etc. are not explicitly in the equations. Thus, if the values of these attributes change for various dwelling types, it will not be possible to forecast the effects of these changes on demand. The model differs from Quigley's [140] who also used the minimum gross price concept but *did* include some other dwelling attributes.

The calculation of gross rents is based on the summation of several components. These are the gross monthly rents for the structure, formulated by the Structure Rent Submodel, a work trip travel cost component which includes valuation of travel time at 40% of the wage rate, an estimate of the cost of non-work trips, and a discrimination markup for black households.

After each moving household has been assigned probabilisticly to a dwelling type, households so assigned are added by type of household to determine the demands for the dwelling types. At the same time, other submodels have generated the dwelling units of each type in each residence zone which are available for occupancy. This is done by adding the units vacated by movers and those newly constructed less those abandoned, demolished, etc. and less some representing normal vacancies. These available units by dwelling type and geographic zone represent the supply offered for occupancy. The next important step in the NBER model is to match the households choosing a dwelling type (or submarket) to the available units in the various geographic zones of that submarket. This is done by solving the following Hitchcock linear program for each dwelling type (50 times in the Pittsburgh and Chicago versions). For each dwelling type k:

$$\underset{\{X^k_{ijh}\}}{\text{Minimize}} \sum_{ijh} C_{ijh} X^k_{ijh}$$

$$\sum_j X^k_{ijh} = D^k_{ih}, \quad \text{each} \quad (i, h);$$

$$\sum_i \sum_h X^k_{ijh} = A^k_j, \quad \text{each} \quad j$$

$$X^k_{ijh} \geq 0 \quad \text{all} \quad (i, j, h, k).$$

Here h denotes the household type and i the workplace of that household type, with D^i_{ih} the demand or total number of (i, h) households assigned to type k dwellings via the multinomial logit model. X^k_{ijh} is then the number of type (i, h) households to be assigned to geographic zone j (and type k dwellings to which they have already been assigned). The objective function coefficients C_{ijh} are costs consisting of four components added together. These are the cost of traveling from workplace i to residence zone j for type h households, the cost of the household's nonwork trips originating in the residence zone j, discrimination costs incurred by black households to obtain a dwelling in the residence zone j, and a cost discount which depends on neighborhood quality and household income. It must be true, to have a nonempty feasible set, that total demand and availability are equal. This requires,

$$\sum_{ih} D^k_{ih} = \sum_j A^k_j.$$

In the NBER model this equality holds by the creation of just enough fictitious households (one of the types (i, h)) when there is excess supply or by the creation of just enough fictitious dwelling units in a fictitious zone (one of the zones j) when there is excess demand. Fictitious households are assigned zero costs for all j and are thus assigned (in the optimal solution) to those residence zones which are least preferred by the actual households. Fictitious dwellings are assigned higher costs than any available unit and are interpreted as locations outside the metropolitan area or expensive quarters such as hotel rooms or accommodations with friends and relatives.

The linear programming solution as we discussed in Part 3, has been shown by Anderson [15] to be equivalent to a special case of the Herbert–Stevens [83] model in which dwellings differ only by location and thus transport costs. The shadow rent, r_{ik}, produced by the linear program, is then used to update the structure rents to be used in the next simulation period. This is done by the equation

$$R_{ik}^t = (0.75)V_{ik}^{t-1} + (0.25)r_{ik}^{t-1} + q_k^t$$

where R_{ik}^t is the structure rent at time t, V_{ik}^{t-1} is the location rent representing the land portion of total rent at time $t - 1$, and r_{ik}^{t-1} is the shadow rent obtained from the linear program. Finally, q_k^t is a quasi-rent for structure type k adjusted according to excess demand or excess supply for type k dwelling in time $t - 1$. For example, for every one percentage point excess demand (supply), the quasi-rent is adjusted up (down) one percentage point from the last period. The coefficients 0.75, 0.25 help set up an adaptive expectations function such that

$$(0.75)V_{ik}^{t-1} + (0.25)r_{ik}^{t-1} = V_{ik}^t.$$

Finally, the structure rents R_{ik}^t are adjusted by adding the appropriate race and other household and workplace specific premia to obtain the gross prices to be used in the next simulation period.

The above discussion completes the central and most important part of the NBER model, which is the demand allocation followed by the market assignment. Because of the model's very large size, the designers are forced to use these two procedures hierarchically, sacrificing some realism and introducing a model structure which departs so much from theory that its performance is somewhat unpredictable.

On the supply side the NBER model has submodels for new construction, conversion of structures from one type to another, maintenance and rehabilitation of structures and demolition and abandonment as well as temporary vacancies. These computations are guided by the profit margins of various structures and dwellings in different locations and also by the expectations of landlords for future market conditions.

The main difficulty with evaluating the NBER model is the complexity introduced by the assumption of disequilibrium and recursively adjusted prices. Economic theory says little about how *urban* markets clear in disequilibrium. There are some recent empirical studies of the housing market in disequilibrium (Anas and Eum [12, 13]). The second of these papers is a first application of the Fair–Jaffee [51] model of market disequilibrium to a spatially disaggregated urban housing market. The authors show that up to 75% of the variance in prices unexplained by the equilibrium models can be explained by lagged variables such as market information and interest rates. In the absence of external shocks prices are shown to stabilize to their equilibrium values within two years.

The central question I wish to address is this: had the designers of the NBER model put together a different but equally plausible procedure for price adjustment and market clearing would they have ended up with substantially different model behavior? I suspect that the answer to this question is "yes." Therefore, we are faced with the epistemological question: how do we know that the NBER procedures are appropriate or realistic enough? To put it another way, what are the hidden qualitative properties of the NBER model, how free are these properties from the sequencing of the various submodels and from the empirically determined coefficients? Although I cannot answer these questions, I can cite the model's findings in support of my conjecture that the answer is too complicated. In the Pittsburgh and Chicago simulations [93] the authors tested the effects of giving housing allowances to low income households in low quality dwellings. They did ten year (1965–1975) baseline simulations (without allowances) and ten year policy simulations (with allowances). They found that average rents in Pittsburgh and Chicago declined to 98 and 99 percent of their baseline levels one year after the policy and to 97 percent of their baseline levels in both cities by 1970. According to theory *and* according to simulation models rooted in theory such as the Urban Institute Model, the effect of allowances is to increase rather than decrease rents. The NBER model finds that rents in part of the stock are increased, decreasing in another part, the latter dominating the former. Presumably the declines occur where allowance recipients move out of low quality or substandard housing. While some of this stock may become occupied by new households who are not recipients (I do not know whether this indeed occurs in the model) most of it becomes vacant, abandoned or demolished.

The authors attempt a plausible but inconclusive explanation for the result of lower rents. They do emphasize the possibility of experimental error based on the selected coefficients. Yet the exact reasons for this result which diverges from the theory remain in doubt because the implications of the model structure are not easy to understand. If the theory is correct then the NBER model structure needs to be revised. But where in the model and how are such revisions to be made? On the other hand, if the NBER model is correct how is the lesson of this model to be translated into improvements in theory? To come up with the answers to these questions we need a theory of the NBER model. What I mean by this is a small analytically tractable version of the model which makes its operation more transparent.

More recently the NBER model (or HUDS as it is now known) has been applied to the evaluation of "Concentrated Housing and Neighborhood Improvement Strategies," more specifcly the revitalization of central city neighborhoods [94]. In these Chicago simulations, Kain and Apgar evaluate a number of strategies and take a very comprehensive view of their effects. Neighborhood and housing improvement subsidies are examined with respect to their impacts on (a) housing production and investment decisions, (b) neighborhood quality and incomes, (c) reduction in abandonments, and (d) gentrification and displacement. They conclude that the policies are beneficial, by comparing baseline and policy simulations. Their findings for different neighborhoods vary greatly in quantitative terms and are very sensitive to the magnitude of the improvement programs. It is difficult to evaluate the model's performance in this particular case, because urban economic theory says little about the dynamics of change in different neighborhood types.

4.3. The Chicago Area Transportation–Land Use Analysis System

The Chicago Area Transportation–Land Use Analysis System or (CATLAS) was developed at Northwestern University during 1980–83 [6]. The model is estimable from census data for the United States and is thus applicable to any large or moderate sized U.S. urban area. However, the only application to date has been for the Chicago metropolitan area. See Anas [6] and Anas and Duann [11].

CATLAS is designed to evaluate the impacts of transportation changes (in any of several modes) on housing values, vacancies, new residential contruction, demolitions and commuters' choices of modes of travel and residence zone by workplace. The model operates for a sequence of annual periods and computes the following for each year and geographic zone. (1) The average housing rent, (2) the number of vacant dwellings, (3) the number of commuters choosing each travel mode and zone of residence by their zone of employment, (4) the number of new dwellings built and old ones demolished, (5) the price and amount of the vacant land, (6) the changes in aggregate housing and land rent (or producer surplus) and consumer surplus for each commuter group by workplace.

In the Chicago application there are four travel modes (auto, bus, rail transit, and commuter rail), two workplaces (downtown or central business district containing 20% of the jobs in 1970 and all other workplaces aggregated together), and 1690 small residential zones of 1/4 square mile to one square mile in size. Workplace disaggregation and the disaggregation of the housing stock by dwelling types can be introduced without entailing any change in the model's structure or an increase in the number of equations. The Chicago application was estimated using data from the 1970 census data and some data from the 1960–1970 decennial changes.

CATLAS consists of a number of equations to be solved simultaneously for each year in a simulation, while some of the variables entering these equations are adjusted recursively from the solution of the previous period. The simulation year is denoted by $t = 1 \ldots T$, the residence zones by $i = 1 \ldots I$, the zones of employment by $h = 1 \ldots H$ and the number of modes available in each zone by $m = 1 \ldots M_i$.

The model's structure is completely described by the following equation system for $i = 1 \ldots I$.

$$\sum_{h=1}^{H} N_h^t \sum_{m=1}^{M_i} \delta_i P_{im}^h(\bar{R}^t, \bar{X}^{Dt}, \bar{Y}_h^t, \bar{\alpha}_h) = S_i^t Q_i^e(R_i^t, \bar{X}_i^{St}, \bar{\beta}); \qquad (1)$$

$$S_i^t = S_i^{t-1} + C_i^{t-1} - D_i^{t-1}; \qquad (2)$$

$$C_i^{t-1} = \left(\frac{L_i^{t-1}}{g_i}\right) Q_i^c(R_{is}^{t-1}, s = 1 \ldots Z; \bar{X}^{St-1}, r, \bar{\gamma}); \tag{3}$$

$$D_i^{t-1} = O_i^{t-1} Q_i^d(R_{is}^{t-1}, s = a_i^{t-1} \ldots Z, \bar{X}^{St-1}, r, \bar{\lambda}); \tag{4}$$

$$L_i^{t-1} = L_i^{t-2} - g_i C_i^{t-2} + g_i D_i^{t-2}; \tag{5}$$

$$O_i^{t-1} = O_i^{t-2} - D_i^{t-2} + A_i^{t-2}; \tag{6}$$

$$R_{is}^{t-1} = R_i^{t-1} + \theta(s - (X_{i1}^{Dt-1})); \tag{7}$$

$$\bar{X}_i^{Dt} = f_1(\bar{X}_i^{Dt-1}); \tag{8}$$

$$\bar{X}_i^{St} = f_2(\bar{X}_i^{St-1}). \tag{9}$$

Equations (1) state that the demand in numbers of households for each geographic zone i is equal to the supply in number of dwellings offered for rent. N_h^t is the given number of jobs in employment zone h at time t, δ_i is zone i's *given* households-to-commuters ratio and $P_{im}^h(\ .\ )$ is the expected proportion of h-commuters who will choose zone i and mode m. These choices are a function of the rents of all the zones, $\bar{R}^t$, of zonal demand side characteristics $\bar{X}^{Dt}$, and of travel time, cost and other transportation characteristics, $\bar{Y}_h^t$. The vector $\bar{\alpha}_h$ contains the estimated coefficients. S_i^t is the number of dwellings in zone i at time t and $Q_i^e(\ .\ )$ is the expected proportion that will be occupied. This depends on zonal rent R_i^t, supply side zonal characteristics $\bar{X}_i^{St}$ and the vector of coefficients $\bar{\beta}$. Equations (1) incorporate the assumption that the existing stock prices equilibrate within a year. Thus these equations are solved each year for the zonal rents $\bar{R}^t$ given the other variables which appear in them.

Equations (2) simply update the housing stock in each zone by adding new dwellings C_i^{t-1}, constructed during $t - 1$ and subtracting D_i^{t-1}, dwellings demolished during $t - 1$. Equations (3) compute new constructions as follows. The land available, L_i^{t-1}, is divided by, g_i, the lot size permissible by zoning regulations, to find (L_i^{t-1}/g_i) the maximum potential number of dwellings that can be accommodated in zone i during $t - 1$. This is multiplied by $Q_i^c(\ .\ )$ which computes the expected proportion of these dwellings that will be built. This is done on the basis of present value calculations over the lifetime Z of new dwellings, r being the interest rate and $\bar{\gamma}$ a vector of estimated coefficients. Equations (4) computes the expected dwellings to be demolished, D_i^{t-1}, as the unprofitable proportion of old dwellings, O_i^{t-1}, which are thirty or more years in age, the average age in the zone being $a_i^{t-1} \geq 30$. $\bar{\lambda}$ is a vector of estimated coefficients. Equations (5) update the available land by adding that released by demolitions and subtracting that taken up by new construction. Equations (6) update the number of old dwellings by subtracting demolitions and adding, A_i^{t-2}, those which age into the "old" category. Equations (7) determine the rent which is expected (at time $t-1$) to accrue to the average dwelling in zone i when that dwelling is s years old or $(s - X_{i1}^{Dt-1})$ years from now, X_{i1}^{Dt-1} being the age of the average dwelling i zone i. Finally Eqs. (8) and (9) adjust the values of some of the zonal variables such as dwelling ages.

In CATLAS, owner and renter occupied dwellings are grouped together, so that letting $t = 0$, the initial year, the average zonal rents are computed by,

$$R_i^o = f_i^o r_i^o + (1 - f_i^o)V_i^o/10$$

where f_i^o is the proportion of the zone's occupied dwellings which are renter occupied dwellings, r_i^o the annual rental and V_i^o the value of the owner occupied dwellings. This equation reflects Shelton's rule [151] which assumes that owners should be imputed rents at one tenth the value of their home.

CATLAS has four behavioral submodels. These are (a) the demand submodel, $P_{im}^i(\ .\ )$; (b) the occupancy–vacancy submodel, $Q_i^e(\ .\ )$; (c) the new construction submodel, $Q_i^c(\ .\ )$; (d) the demolition submodel, $Q_i^d(\ .\ )$. Each of these is a logit model appropriately derived from the utility or profit maximization. The equations are as follows:

$$P_{im}^h = P_i^h \cdot P_{m|i}^h$$

where

$$P_{m|i}^h = \exp(U_{im}^h) \bigg/ \sum_{n=1}^{M_i} \exp(U_{in}^h)$$

is the mode choice model conditional on zone choice with the utility of mode choice given as,

$$U_{im}^h = \alpha_2^h \log(R_i + C_{im}^h) + \bar{\alpha}_3^h \bar{Y}_{im}^h, \qquad \alpha_2^h < 0.$$

where C_{im}^h is the cost of commuting by mode m. The marginal zone choice model is,

$$P_i^h = S_i^{\alpha_o^h} \exp[U_i^h + (1 - \alpha_1^h)I_i^h] \Big/ \sum_{j=1}^{I} S_j^{\alpha_o^h} \exp[U_j^h + (1 - \alpha_1^h)I_j^h].$$

This is a nested logit model with $0 < \alpha_o^h < 1$ and α_1^h, the inclusive value coefficient also between zero and one. The inclusive value defined as the expected maximum utility of the mode choice decision is given by

$$I_i^h = \log \sum_{m=1}^{M_i} \exp(U_{im}^h)$$

and the zone utility U_i^h is given by,

$$U_i^h = \bar{\alpha}_4^h \bar{X}_i^D.$$

The vacancy–occupancy submodel is derived from annual binary profit maximization, recognizing that the owner of an existing dwelling will postpone selling or renting in the current period if the differential maintenance cost of an occupied versus vacant dwelling exceeds the rent that can be obtained that year. The binary choice probability $Q_i^e(\ . \ )$ is given by

$$Q_i^e = \frac{\exp(\beta_0 R_i + \sum_{n=1}^N \beta_n X_{in}^s)}{1 + \exp(\beta_o R_i + \sum_{n=1}^N \beta_n X_{in}^s)}$$

where $\beta_o > 0$ and the summation approximates differential maintenance costs as a function of zonal supply side characteristics.

The new construction submodel computes, $Q_i^{ct}(\ . \ )$ the probability that a vacant lot will be developed during period t by comparing the present value of expected profits if the lot is developed to the present value of expected profits if the lot remains vacant. Again this is a binary choice and differential costs are made functions of zonal characteristics. Thus,

$$Q_i^{ct} = \frac{\exp[\gamma_o(PVR)_{ti1} + \sum_{n=1}^N \gamma_n X_{in}^{St}]}{1 + \exp[\gamma_o(PVR)_{ti1} + \sum_{n=1}^N \gamma_n X_{in}^{St}]}$$

with $\gamma_0 > 0$ and $(PVR)_{ti1}$ is the present value of the new dwelling's expected revenue computed as,

$$(PVR)_{ti1} = \sum_{s=1}^{Z} \frac{R_{is}^t Q_{is}^{et}(\ \cdot \ )}{(1+r)^{s-1}}$$

The case of demolition probabilities is similar. They are given by $Q_i^{dt}(\ \cdot \ )$:

$$Q_i^{dt} = \frac{1}{1 + \exp[\lambda_o(PVR)_{ti} + \sum_{n=1}^{N} \lambda_n X_{in}^{St}]}$$

where $\lambda_0 > 0$ and $(PVR)_{ti}$ is the "present value of revenue over the remaining lifetime of the average old dwelling in zone i, at time t." This is,

$$(PVR)_{ti} = \sum_{s=a_i^t}^{Z} \frac{R_{is}^t Q_{is}^{et}(\ \cdot \ )}{(1+r)^{s-1}}$$

In [6], numerical simulations over a twenty year period demonstrate that the annual predictions converge to steady state limit cycles and with a constant population (constant total demand) excess vacancies are reduced to zero. An algorithm is developed [4; Ch. 5] and shown to efficiently compute the solution to the 1690 equations in (1) for each year t.

The demand, occupancy and new construction submodels are estimated directly from the 1970 census using maximum likelihood techniques, whereas the coefficients of the demolition submodel are fitted to approximate annual demolition rates for the entire metropolitan area estimated from decade-long trends for the sixties.

CATLAS has been used to test the effects of rapid transit investment policy in Chicago's Southwest corridor for a radial line connecting the CBD with the inner suburbs. These simulations show that such a new line competes mostly with existing bus lines but also captures some trips from auto commuting. It results in low ridership and fare revenues are insufficient to cover operating and costs. The investment lowers rents in the city because it enables some city residents to move out to suburban locations and others to move closer to the transit line. Suburban rents are raised on the average. However, these effects are extremely unevenly distributed geographically. A few neighborhoods near transit stations can experience annual rent appreciation per dwelling of up to about

$250. Decreases begin to occur a few miles away and are very small: only a few dollars per dwelling annually. While these decreases can add up over the entire metropolitan area to create an overall negative effect on aggregate rents, they are so small on a per capita basis that may be ignored from the point of view of levying a special compensatory assessment. *Within the Southwest corridor,* it was found that the proposed investments raised rents an average of 2–3% in the city and an average of 0.7% in the suburbs. The average per dwelling annual increase within the corridor was about $26, a very modest special assessment burden. Levying such special assessments as one time lump sum taxes on the current owners of housing and vacant land was shown to raise up to 40% of the capital cost of the least expensive of the proposed transit lines. This figure is much higher than the Carter administration's expectation that local areas should raise up to 15% of the capital costs of such investments. Since transit ridership tends to decline when fares are raised sharply, the above housing based taxation approach (known as value capture) is shown to be a more effective finance technique. Furthermore, it may be argued that inclusion of commercial real estate and some other factors lacking from the model would make the cost recovery ratio even higher.

These policy results are of strictly quantitative nature. It is impossible to gain sufficient insight, from simpler models, into the magnitudes of cost recovery ratios or the magnitudes of their associated average tax burdens. The selection of such problems of inherently empirical quantitative interest is the most fertile ground for large scale urban simulation models.

4.4. A model of regulated european housing markets

While housing markets in the United States are essentially free of government controls, in Western Europe and Scandinavia the pricing, trading and supply of housing is subject to extensive, sometimes severe government regulation. In these countries, "mixed housing markets" prevail: part of the stock is freely priced and traded and the other part is subject to varying degrees of government control and regulation.

Economic and regulatory behavior in the housing markets of these nations has not been adequately modeled. An attempt in this direction is by Weibull [173]. He builds a simple numerical model of a housing market with two sectors. In one of these sectors prices are free and housing is traded competitively and without trade frictions (transaction costs). In the other sector, prices are fixed by regulation and excess demands are dissipated by means of trade frictions causing spillovers to the unregulated sector. The model produces the following comparative statics: If the regulated price (regulated stock) of dwellings is increased, prices in the freely traded sector are increased (decreased) and the frictions in the regulated sector are reduced. It is known from theory, however, that if an explicit rationing procedure is used to dissipate trade frictions, then an increase in the regulated price could also result in a decrease in the prices of the freely traded sector.

Weibull's model contains a number of limitations. The utility maximizing behavior of the housing consumer, the profit maximizing behavior of the landlords or the government's regulatory behavior are not explicitly treated. Homeownership and rental are not distinguished and the creation of vacancies as a result of mobility decisions is not explicit. Policy instruments such as taxes and housing allowances are not in the model and the actual institutional structure of a specific regulated market is not of concern. Also, the model does not contain welfare measures and cannot identify policy or institutional changes which result in Pareto improvements.

Taking the institutional structure of the Swedish housing market as a given, Anas and Cho [9] have recently developed a model which incorporates the above features. The utility maximizing behavior of households is developed in a discrete-time mobility context and the households' choice probabilities for various transaction options are derived in multinomial logit form as in the CATLAS model (see [6]). The place of policy instruments in these probabilities is explicitly determined. Households' behavior in letting vacancies in the legal and subletting in the black markets is also explicitly defined. The landlord's (housing company's) or public authority's behavior in rationing dwellings at fixed prices is modeled as a stochastic rationing process which matches households and dwellings and generates queue waiting times. Rationing is influenced by economic criteria such as short run profits in the face of vacancies and, in the case of the public authority, by socioeconomic priority weights. A marginal calculus is assumed where an additional match takes place as long as its marginal benefit exceeds its marginal cost. The model's equations are assembled into a framework of simultaneous equations which equate effective demands and effective supplies. Solving these equations yields free market prices for the freely traded stock, black market premia for the illegally traded stock, side payments exchanged between owners or tenants swapping dwellings (a common transaction method in Sweden) and waiting times incurred in securing a regulated dwelling from nonprofit companies or the public housing authority. The model also determines vacancies, the spillover of households from the regulated to the freely traded part and the mobility of households among various parts of the market via the available transaction options. These options include free buy and sell, black buys and sales, swapping of dwellings and entry of both households and dwellings into the queues of housing companies or the public housing agency.

Comparative statics is used to analyze the direction of change in key endogenous variables in response to changes in key exogenous variables. Compensated equilibria are computed to see if Pareto improvements occur relative to an initial situation when a policy action is introduced. The simulations show that the complex Swedish institutional schemes create a number of counterintuitive, unintended and possibly undesirable effects in the housing market. For example, an increase in the mortgage interest payments of homeowners can increase rather than decrease owner occupied housing prices because many owners qualify for bigger housing allowances which, given the Swedish formulae, can more than offset the effect of higher interest payments. Increasing the fixed regulated rent of apartments has two effects: it depresses the demand for apartments but it increases the landlords' (or government's) willingness to accept applicants because it raises the opportunity cost of a vacancy. When the latter effect dominates the former, the spillover of apartment seekers to other submarkets is mitigated and prices in these other submarkets fall. This effect does not occur in Weibull [173] because rationing behavior is not explicitly modeled by him.

Policy simulations are also used to examine the efficiency of deregulating the Swedish housing market, for example, by eliminating the public rationing of some of the stock. Even though such deregulation favors more competition, it may not yield a Pareto improvement if households experience lower transaction costs by waiting in public queues rather than by searching on their own in the free submarkets.

4.5. A supply side simulation model

Recently, Arnott [16] has reported the ongoing development of HOPSIM (A Housing Policy Simulation Model). This is a model of the competitive housing market in a state of dynamic, perfect foresight equilibrium. The chief contribution of the model, like CATLAS [6], is to elaborate the supply side response of competitive landlord–builders, an aspect treated in ad-hoc fashion in the Urban Institute and NBER models. The stock of housing is described as the floor area available at various quality levels and structural densities. Like CATLAS, in HOPSIM, landlord–builders decide on the volume of housing construction and demolition and, unlike CATLAS, they also decide on how much to spend on maintenance (in the case of rental housing). These supply side aspects of the model are inspired by the theoretical model of Arnott, Davidson and Pines [17, 18]. On the demand side, the model includes a variety of income–demographic groups. Each household takes rents and values as given and decides for every time period whether to rent or own. Renters decide how much housing of what quality to rent and owner-occupiers decide how much housing of what quality to buy and also how much to spend on maintenance.

Early development of the model was financially supported by the Canada Mortgage and Housing Corporation. Full econometric development and testing has not yet occurred and a solid computational procedure remains to be developed. Eventually, HOPSIM may be a powerful tool for testing the dynamic effects of housing policies under assumptions of rational expectations.

5. REGIONAL AND INTERREGIONAL MODELS

My comments in the introduction to this article lamented the lack of a microeconomic theory of the regional and interregional economy. It was also pointed out in the introduction that the theory of city systems currently pioneered by urban economists [80, 82] could eventually form the basis of an adequate interregional theory. Another source of inspiration and theoretical insight for regional and interregional models ought to come from "applied general equilibrium analysis" which in recent years has found many topics of economic policy application with major reliance on numerical computation techniques. A collection of such articles appears in the volume edited by Scarf and Shoven [147]. In one of these articles, Kimbell and Harrison [99] develop a nonspatial, two-region general equilibrium economy with an interindustry and interregional trade structure to examine the repercussions of a capital tax reduction such as Proposition 13 in California (the rest-of-the-U.S. being the second region). They find by means of numerical solution of a carefully parametrized model that the tax cut does not strongly propagate to other regions. A somewhat similar and slightly earlier paper is by Beck [25] who examines the effects of a business property tax on interjurisdictional capital mobility. He concludes, for chosen parameter values, that the optimal classified local property tax rate on business property is less than that on residential property. Such representative articles in the general equilibrium tradition define a possible style for future regional and interregional modeling which, however, is not fully adopted by regional economists at the present time.

Because of the lack of a formal theory or a slowness in adapting one from general equilibrium analysis, interregional and regional simulation techniques have been developed somewhat in a vacuum. These techniques have borrowed from macroeconomic theory and from the scientific style of the national econometric studies and models. The purpose of this section is to briefly discuss three major approaches which fall in the category of regional and interregional models for economic simulation. These are: (a) regional and interregional input output models, (b) regional econometric models, (c) regional–metropolitan models with intrametropolitan geographic disaggregation, and (d) models of less developed nations.

5.1. Regional and interregional input–output

It is beyond the scope of this article to survey the vast literature on input–output models. The application of these models to economic forecasting are more routine and better understood than any other model discussed in this article. Therefore, it will be more useful to focus on the less well understood deficiencies of input–output models.

A general statement of the input–output model as developed by Leontieff [109] and Isard [89, 90] is as follows. The model states that

$$X = (I - A)^{-1} Y$$

where X is the vector containing the total output of each industry in each region and Y is the vector containing the output of each industry in each region needed for final consumption in that region. Both X and Y are measured in value terms rather than in physical quantities. A is the square Leontieff matrix of technical production and trade coefficients. More precisely $A \triangleq [A_{ij}^{kl}]$ where a_{ij}^{kl} is the proportion of the value of the output of the jth industry in region 1 contributed by purchases of inputs from the ith industry in region k. Thus,

$$a_{ij}^{kl} = x_{ij}^{kl} / X_j^l$$

where x_{ij}^{kl} is the value of the output of industry i in region k purchased by industry j in region l and X_j^l is the value of the total output of industry j in region l. When $l = k$, then the input–output coefficient measures a production relationship. The underlying technology is based on the assumption that these coefficients remain constant. When $k \neq l$ then the coefficient measures a trade relationship as well as a production relationship. These coefficients are crucial in an interregional input–output model and they are also assumed to remain constant. Thus, the trade and production technologies are assumed to conform to a fixed coefficient constant returns to scale process: no substitution of one input for another or of one trade origin for another is allowed.

This very strong assumption in input–output models is actually much more serious when one takes into account the fact that output and interindustry flows are measured in value as opposed to physical terms. Nevertheless, the severity of these assumptions were not clearly articulated in writing until 1974 in a presidential address delivered to the Regional Science Association by Moses [131]. To see the logic of this critique we will first define the interindustry flows as,

$$x_{ij}^{kl} = q_{ij}^{kl} P_i^k$$

where q_{ij}^{kl} is the physical quantity of the output of industry i in region k purchased by industry j in region l and P_i^k is the price of one unit of this output. By the same definition, industry output is,

$$X_j^l = Q_j^l P_j^l$$

where Q_j^l is the physical output of industry j in region l and P_j^l is the price of this output. Now our input–output coefficients can be written as

$$a_{ij}^{kl} = \left(\frac{q_{ij}^{kl}}{Q_j^l}\right)\left(\frac{P_i^k}{P_j^l}\right).$$

The first ratio on the right side is the ratio of the traded physical input used in the production of the total physical output of the purchasing industry. The second ratio is the price of the input relative to the price of the output. We can thus see that the constancy of the value based coefficients requires the constancy of the technological coefficients but also the constancy of relative prices. While the assumption that production functions are constant over the short or medium run because of no technological change may be tenable, the additional assumption that relative prices are also constant is clearly untenable even for the short run. Furthermore, if these prices are not constant there should be substitution in trade if not in production.

There are other problems with input–output analysis. The model assumes that final demands, $\bar{Y}$, must be forecasted independently and then the economy's production levels, $\bar{X}$, computed from these final demands. Actually, consumption decisions by government, households, etc. must be determined simultaneously with investment and production decisions together with all the prices in the economy, following a general equilibrium analysis.

While these criticisms appear quite decisive from the point-of-view of general equilibrium economics, input–output techniques have been extensively studied and applied primarily because the data needed for more sophisticated models is not easily accessible.

The best known regional input–output study is for the Philadelphia region. In this study the input–output table was used to estimate the impact of the Vietnam war on the Philadelphia economy by specifying certain government purchases as final demands for the region's output in certain war related industries (see Isard and Langford [91]).

5.2. Regional econometric models

The idea of a regional (macro)econometric model is similar in style and spirit to the concept of a national (macro)econometric model. Perhaps the best known such model is the Wharton Annual and Long-Term Econometric Model [137]. Such a model conceives the national economy as an economic system linked to the outside world through imports, exports, foreign aid and the like. Model equations are usually linear or linearized functions that can be estimated via well established econometric techniques such as two stage least squares. These equations describe the interrelationships among the economy's industries grouped appropriately as well as the consumption and investment sectors, including public expenditure and investment. Unlike input–output, these models did not emerge fully formulated from the start but have been evolved over perhaps three decades or more from a single macro-behavioral relationship: the consumption function and its associated accounting identity.

A chief characteristic of these models is their painstakingly careful relationship to available data and in particular to monthly or quarterly time series data on many variables. Also important is the consistency of these models with national accounts.

Project LINK which has been ongoing at the University of Pennsylvania represents another level in macro modeling. It attempts to combine the national econometric models of several countries in order to simulate issues in international trade and the response of nations to global developments.

The idea of a regional econometric model originates with papers by Klein [102] and Glickman [65] the latter of whom is primarily responsible for developing the econometric model of the Philadelphia region. A later paper by Klein and Glickman [103] assesses the scope, ambitions and prospects of econometric model building at the regional level. The authors' view is motivated by the relatively great lack of data at the regional level. A region may be defined as a metropolitan area, a group of countries, a state, a group of states or a more functionally defined spatial area. No matter which definition is used regional accounts and time series are rarely if ever complete and the import–export flows linking the region to the rest of the nation can rarely be fully constructed. There are also difficulties with assigning to a region entities such as corporate profits since many corporations operate their various activities in a number of regions and even nations rather than in one. These difficulties notwithstanding there have been numerous attempts at building econometric models of regions and states. In his book, Glickman [66] counts fifteen simultaneous equation models for states, large metropolitan areas or parts of a state. Glickman's own Philadelphia model [65] consists of 288 equations and 19 industrial groups. This is larger and more disaggregated than most regional models and compares well in size with national models which often have more than one hundred equations. In most other cases, however, data limitations force models with less than 35 equations.

Klein and Glickman [103] offer two views for the role of these aggregative regional models. The first view is to treat and solve these models as "satellites" of the national model. Some of the endogenous variables of a national model such as interest rates, unemployment, wage levels etc. will be taken by the regional model as exogeneous and this model will be used to solve for regional economic activity and the regional values of the exogenous national variables. This top-to-bottom econometrics contrasts with the second view: bottom-to-top econometrics which treats the national model itself as nothing more than an integrated system of completely specified regional models much in the same way as project LINK strives for a global model by linking various national models. The latter approach is difficult to implement because of the data problems at the regional level. Nevertheless, Klein and Glickman [103] express the expectation that when there is an econometric model of each of the United States an attempt may be made to link them into a national model. Until such time, the satellite view remains dominant.

Regional econometric models treat the region as an aggregate, although in some cases, as in the Philadelphia model, there is a division of the region into city and suburbs. No attention is paid, in any of these models, to actual land use or spatial structure within the regions.

A point not emphasized by Klein and Glickman [103] is the fact that the structure of these models follows closely (indeed mimicks) the present industrial composition of a region. As such they are especially short term forecasting tools. These models cannot be used to explain adequately an emerging or changing industrial structure. However, as I explained in the introduction, an inter-regional theory which is essentially microeconomic could potentially do so.

5.3. Regional intra-metropolitan models

With regional econometric models on one side and land use oriented econometric models of a metropolitan area on the other side, there is a logical place for the development of a model type that links the two.

This was the apparent mission of the Engle–Fisher–Harris–Rothenberg model [50] of the Boston region. More than an actual model, the authors have developed a sketch of what a model would ideally look like. At the intra-metropolitan level they attempted to construct the interaction of the housing, business, transportation and local government sectors, a feature which was not included in any of the econometric models discussed in Section 4.

The authors proposed three interconnected models: a macro-economic nonspatial model of regional output, employment and income distribution (operating as a regional econometric model linkable to a national model), a model of long term adjustments of population and capital stocks, and a model of land use allocation. They envisaged a spatial disaggregation scheme whereby each zone in the model corresponded to a jurisdication in the Boston region with equations in place to simulate the fiscal budgets of these jurisdictions and to determine tax rates.

The proposed feedback and interactions among the three sub-models has been described by the authors as follows [50; p. 88].

The macroeconomic model takes as given: population, capital stock, technology, external demand, wages, prices, and unemployment. It generates output, employment, wages and prices, and an income distribution for the city. The longterm adjustments consist of population change and migration and capital investment in industry which respond partly to conditions in Boston and partly to conditions within the rest of the nation. These two submodels taken together provide an aggregative growth model of the metropolis as a given economy. Their outputs are primary inputs into the spatial allocation model. The latter takes the population of households and businesses along with existing stocks of structures and determines the locational patterns among the many political jurisdictions and subjurisdictions of the metropolitan area. Within this submodel, changes in location patterns as well as changes in population and income give rise to adjustment of the stock of structures via construction, filtering, and demolition. Public services and tax rates (which may later be modelled as endogenous) affect the location of activities. Feedback from the spatial–allocation submodel to the macro and long-term adjustment submodels occurs through housing and land prices and average tax rates.

Although the Engle–Fisher–Harris–Rothenberg model has not been implemented to any degree of completeness it remains the only careful statement of the manner in which regional econometric and spatially disaggregated models may be combined in some future research.

5.4. Models of less developed nations

Economic and urban development in the less developed nations of the third world remains an important but still relatively poorly understood subject. A seminal paper that attracted attention to this area and proposed a theoretical model was by Harris and Todaro [74], published in 1970. The authors noted the phenomenon of extensive rural to urban migration despite positive marginal products in agriculture and high levels of unemployment. They explained this phenomenon by postulating that the urban formal sector offered a relatively inflexible wage, much above the minimal agricultural wage. This causes the rational rural to urban migrant to be driven by *expected earnings* at the risk of accepting unemployment. Therefore, the probability of remaining unemployed (or unemployment rate) acted as an equilibrating variable on the migration. This theoretical perspective generates some testable hypotheses and is a refreshing counterpart to the treatment of migration by demographers as exogenous.

Since the Harris–Todaro model, there has been considerable interest in modeling analytically various aspects of growth in less developed nations. A concerted and comprehensive effort is by Kelley and Williamson [95, 96, 97] who developed a computable dynamic general equilibrium model of a "representative developing country" or RDC. Their prototype model contains eight sectors each of which is either urban or rural. Each sector produces a commodity or service which is either tradeable internationally, tradeable internally or nontradeable. Agriculture is a rural sector and manufacturing an urban sector, both producing internationally tradeable goods. Formal urban services (a sector which stands primarily for infrastructure) is traded interregionally and produces its output with a production function which utilizes capital and highly skilled labor. The other sectors are rural and urban informal service sectors, a rural housing sector and high and low cost urban housing sectors all of which produce nontradeable goods. Traditional capital, labor (skilled and unskilled) and land are primary factors of production. Production functions also take imported goods (such as fuel) and intermediate goods as additional inputs. The nation is assumed to be a price taker in both imports and exports where finished product prices are determined exogeneously by world conditions (economic and political). The model distinguishes value-added and tariff-distorted prices.

Other interesting aspects of the Kelley–Williamson model is the use of Cobb–Douglas and nested constant elasticity of substitution production functions, their assumption that capital is sector-specific and remains immobile once allocated to a sector, their treatment of education, training and skill formation and their inclusion of the competition for land between urban housing and agriculture. Finally, balance of payments and foreign trade is taken into account and a government sector which levies a variety of taxes is specified. The model being dynamic, household savings, housing investment and aggregate saving, capital accumulation and depreciation are also explicitly treated.

In summary the Kelley–Williamson model is quite complex. The static version contains seventy eight parameters and generates predictions on more than one hundred endogenous variables. Thus the ratio of exogenous variables plus parameters to endogenous variables is fairly high. The relationships in the model appear to have been painstakingly constructed and are justified and defended by drawing on a vast literature from the field of development economics. In essence, the model emerges as an analytical embodiment of much collective knowledge and empirical research.

The empirical validation of this complex model is at best questionable, but the authors seem to have approached this problem with more thoroughness than past studies in development economics. In [97], they report a validation procedure which works as follows: First, data is pooled for 40 nations from 5 continents to create a prototype RDC. The data covers the period 1960 to the early eighties. This span is divided into the pre-OPEC (1960–1973) and post-OPEC periods with the former forming the basis for validation. The authors show that the pattern of the RDC is closely tracked by the model in terms of all the stylized phenomena of development economics: growth, accumulation, inequality, unbalanced growth, industrialization, migration, city growth, land use and density etc. For the post-OPEC period the model is able to capture the observed retardation in city growth and predicts that city growth would have surged in the absence of OPEC. Projecting up to the year 2000 under various scenarios the authors argue that rural to urban migration and city growth in less developed nations are likely to ease considerably and that the high levels of the seventies were unusually severe.

It is clear that the Kelley–Williamson model sets a unique style for the applied modeling of development in Third World countries. While the model was not applied to a single nation and was thus general in its conclusions, a model of India, inspired in large measure by the same style, has been recently developed by Becker, Mills and Williamson [26]. The model's sectors and construction is very similar to the Kelley–Williamson prototype, but careful attention is also paid to the Indian tax structure.

CONCLUSIONS

In closing, a few words may be said about the possible future of urban and regional economic modeling.

I would conjecture that the monocentric style of analysis has, by now, lost its initial appeal having, however, impacted urban economics in a major way. I would not expect much to occur in the area of "monocentric simulation" but I see the possibility of a new generation of multicentric simulation models setting a new style, which ought to be indispensably linked to numerical analysis. There are two other areas of fruitful research in the future. One of these is the development of mathematical programming models at a level of realism which makes them applicable to real policy oriented planning problems, such as public facility investments, transportation networks or the industrial zoning of land. Within this broad area there is the problem of the development of dynamic models of optimal land use allocation. The second area is the continued development of spatially disaggregated econometric models such as those discussed in Section 4. These are forecasting or market oriented predictive models and the major challenge ahead is to expand them beyond the housing market to include employment location, traffic and local government behavior. Indeed, the last sector is a sorely needed development, as there has been nothing done to build simulation models of local government behavior incorporating the theory of urban public finance.

Both of the above areas stand to benefit greatly from the emergence of new supercomputers and from the growing tendency of public agencies to collect and store data in machine readable form. Yet these two factors are far from enough. The tasks ahead are quite staggering and require much ingenuity and boldness. Perhaps one of the biggest obstacles is the scientific tendency to dwell too long on academic and sometimes obscure problems rather than direct that energy to practical problems of model building. This will become much easier if economics can spawn a generation of applied urban economists and econometricians with well defined values and goals.

The ultimate urban economic model may be described as a model of several private sectors such as industry and housing, firmly rooted in microeconomics and estimated with micro data on firm and household behavior with adequate disaggregation in land use. An essential ingredient in such a model should be the behavior of each jurisdiction determining tax rates and other fiscal variables. Such a model which is capable of forecasting market behavior in conjunction with local public sector behavior can then be embedded into an optimization framework in order to examine the efficiency of the combined market and local public sector system.

Interregional modeling may be envisaged as the linking of complete urban models based on microeconomic theory and general equilibrium much in the same spirit as the linking of regional models or of national models to date has been based on macroeconomics.

The above thoughts are intended to highlight an ideal progression, such as that discussed in the introduction, but, needless to say, actual progress will continue to be guided by data availability, computing technology, and the emergence of public policy "fads."

Acknowledgements

During the preparation of this volume the author received valuable comments and suggestions from Richard Arnott, Masahisa Fujita, Paul Hobson, and David Wildasin. Their comments are appreciated while the author maintains full responsibility for the contents.

References

[1] Abdulaal, M. and L. J. Leblanc, "Continuous Equilibrium Network Design Models," *Transportation Research B*, **13** (1979), 292–314.

[2] Alonso W., *Location and Land Use*, Cambridge, Mass: Harvard Press, 1964.

[3] Anas, A., "Dynamics of Urban Residential Growth," *Journal of Urban Economics*, **5** (1978), 66–87.

[4] Anas, A., *Residential Location Markets and Urban Transportation: Economic Theory, Econometrics and Policy Analysis with Discrete Choice Models*, New York: Academic Press, 1982.

[5] Anas, A., "Discrete Choice Theory, Information Theory and the Multinomial Logit and Gravity Models," *Transportation Research B*, **17** (1983), 13–23.

[6] Anas, A., "The Effects of Transportation on the Tax Base and Development of Cities," U.S. Department of Transportation, University Research Program, DOT/OST/P-30/85/005 (1983).

[7] Anas, A., "Estimation of Stochastic Network Equilibrium Models from Link Flows." Working paper, Evanston: Northwestern University, 1986.

[8] Anas, A. and J. R. Cho, "Existence and Uniqueness of Price Equilibria: Theory and Application to Discrete Choice Models," *Regional Science and Urban Economics*, **16** (1986), 211–239.

[9] Anas, A. and J. R. Cho, "A Dynamic, Policy Oriented Model of the Regulated Housing Market: The Swedish Prototype." Working paper. Evanston: Northwestern University, 1986.

[10] Anas, A. and C. Chu, "Discrete Choice Models and the Housing Price and Travel to Work Elasticities of Location Demand," *Journal of Urban Economics*, **15** (1984), 107–123.

[11] Anas, A. and L. S. Duann, "Dynamic Forecasting of Travel Demand, Residential Location and Land Development," *Papers of the Regional Science Association*, **56** (1985), 35–58.

[12] Anas, A. and S. J. Eum, "Hedonic Analysis of a Housing Market in Disequilibrium," *Journal of Urban Economics*, **15** (1984), 87–106.

[13] Anas, A. and S. J. Eum, "Disequilibrium Models of Single Family Housing Prices and Transactions," *Journal of Urban Economics*, **16** (1986), 75–96.

[14] Anderson, G. S., "A Linear Programming Model of Housing Market Equilibrium," *Journal of Urban Economics*, **11** (1982), 159–168.

[15] Anderson, G. S., "Characteristics of Discrete Housing Market Model Equilibria," *Journal of Urban Economics*, **16** (1984), 125–148.

[16] Arnott, R. J., "HOPSIM: A Housing Policy Simulation Model," (mimeo) Kingston, Ontario: Queen's University 1985.

[17] Arnott, R. J., R. Davidson and D. Pines, "Housing Quality, Maintenance and Rehabilitation," *Review of Economic Studies*, **50** (1983), 467–494.

[18] Arnott, R. J., R. Davidson and D. Pines, "Spatial Aspects of Housing Quality, Density and Maintenance," *Journal of Urban Economics*, **19** (1986), 190–217.

[19] Arnott, R. J. and J. G. MacKinnon, "Measuring the Costs of Height Restrictions with a General Equilibrium Model," *Journal of Regional Science and Urban Economics*, **7** (1977), 359–376.

[20] Arnott, R. J. and J. G. MacKinnon, "The Effects of Urban Transportation Changes: A General Equilibrium Simulation," *Journal of Public Economics*, **8** (1977), 389–407.

[21] Arnott, R. J. and J. G. MacKinnon, "The Effects of the Property Tax: A General Equilibrium Simulation," *Journal of Urban Economics*, **4** (1977), 389–407.

[22] Arnott, R. J. and J. G. MacKinnon, "Market and Shadow Land Rents with Congestion," *American Economic Review*, **68** (1978), 588–600.

[23] Arnott, R. J., J. G. MacKinnon and W. C. Wheaton, "The Welfare Implications of Spatial Interdependence: A Extension of Wheaton's 'Optimal Distribution of Income Among Cities'," *Journal of Urban Economics*, **5** (1978), 131–136.

[24] Batty, M., *Urban Modeling: Algorithms, Calibrations, Predictions*, Cambridge: Cambridge University Press, 1976.

[25] Beck, J. H., "Tax Competition, Uniform Assessment and the Benefit Principle," *Journal of Urban Economics*, **13** (1983), 127–146.

[26] Becker, C., E. S. Mills and J. G. Williamson, "Public Policy, Urbanization and Development: A Computable General Equilibrium Model of the Indian Economy." Working Paper No. 83-W14, Department of Economics, Vanderbilt University, 1983.

[27] Beckmann, M. J., "Principles of Optimum Location for Transportation Networks" in *Quantitative Geography, Part I: Economic and Cultural Topics*, ed. by W. L. Garrison, D. F. Marble, Northwestern University, Evanston, (1967), 95–119.

[28] Beckmann, M. J., *Location Theory*. New York: Random House, 1968.

[29] Beckmann, M. J., "On the Distribution of Urban Rent and Residential Density," *Journal of Economic Theory*, **1** (1969), 60–68.

[30] Beckmann, M. J., "Spatial Equilibrium in the Dispersed City," in *Mathematical Land Use Theory*, ed. by G. J. Papageorgiou. Lexington: Lexington Books, 1976.

[31] Beckmann, M., C. B. McGuire and C. B. Winsten, *Studies in the Economics of Transportation*, New Haven: Yale University Press, 1956.

[32] Ben-Akiva, M., A. de Palma and P. Kanaroglou, "Dynamic Model of Peak Period Traffic Congestion with Elastic Arrival Rates," *Transportation Science*, **20** (1986), 164–181.

[33] Ben-Shahar, H., A. Mazor and D. Pines, "Town Planning and Welfare Maximization: A Methodological Approach," *Regional Studies*, **3** (1969), 105–113.

[34] Borukhov, E. and O. Hochman, "Optimum and Market Equilibrium in a Model City without a Predetermined Center," *Environment and Planning A*, **9** (1977), 849–856.

[35] Boyce, D. E., Farhi, A. and R. Weischedel, "Optimal Network Problem: A Branch and Bound Algorithm," *Environment and Planning*, **5** (1973), 519–533.

[36] Boyce, D. E. and B. N. Janson, "A Discrete Transportation Network Design Problem with Combined Trip Distribution and Assignment," *Transportation Research B*, **14** (1980), 147–154.

[37] Carlton, D., "The Location and Employment Choices of New Firms: An Econometric Model with Discrete and Continuous Endogenous Variables," *The Review of Economics and Statistics*, **65** (1983), 440–460.

[38] Dafermos, S. C., "Traffic Assignment and Resource Allocation in Transportation Networks," Ph.D. Dissertation, Department of Operations Research, Johns Hopkins University, Baltimore, 1968.

[39] Daganzo, C., *Multinomial Probit: The Theory and its Application to Demand Forecasting*, New York: Academic Press, 1979.

[40] Daganzo, C. F. and Y. Sheffi, "On Stochastic Models of Traffic Assignment," *Transportation Science*, **11** (1977), 253–274.

[41] Dantzig, G. B., R. P. Harvey, Z. F. Lansdowne, D. W. Robinson, S. F. Maier, "Formulating and Solving the Network Design Problem by Decomposition," *Transportation Research B*, **13** (1979), 5–17.

[42] DeLeeuw, F. and R. J. Struyk, *The Web of Urban Housing: Analyzing Policy with a Market Simulation Model*, Washington, D.C.: The Urban Institute, 1975.

[43] DeLeeuw, F. and R. J. Struyk, "Analyzing Housing Policies with the Urban Institute Housing Model" in *Residential Location and Urban Housing Markets*, ed. by G. K. Ingram, Cambridge: Ballinger, 1977.

[44] Devarajan, S., D. Fullerton, and R. A. Musgrave, "Estimating the Distribution of Tax Burdens: A Comparison of Different Approaches," *Journal of Public Economics*, **13** (1980), 115–182.

[45] Dionne, R. and M. Florian, "Exact and Approximate Algorithms for Optimal Network Design," Publication 41, Centre de Recherche sur les Transports, Montreal: Universite de Montreal, 1977.

[46] Dixit, A., "The Optimum Factory Town," *The Bell Journal of Economics and Management Science*, **4** (1978), 637–651.

[47] Domencich, T. and D. McFadden, *Urban Travel Demand: A Behavioral Analysis*, Amsterdam: North-Holland Publishing Co., 1975.

[48] Eash, R. W., B. N. Janson and D. E. Boyce, "Equilibrium Trip Assignment: Advantages and Implications for Practice," *Transportation Research Record*, **728** (1979), 1–8.

[49] Ellickson, B., "An Alternative Test of the Hedonic Theory of Housing Markets," *Journal of Urban Economics*, **9** (1981), 56–80.

[50] Engle, R. F., F. M. Fisher, J. R. Harris and J. Rothenberg, "An Econometric Simulation of Intra-Metropolitan Location: Housing, Business, Transportation and Local Government," *American Economic Review*, **62** (1972), 87–97.

[51] Fair, R. C. and D. M. Jaffee, "Methods of Estimation for Markets in Disequilibrium," *Econometrica*, **40** (1972), 497–514.

[52] Fisk, C., "Some Developments in Equilibrium Traffic Assignment," *Transportation Research B*, **14** (1980), 243–255.

[53] Florian, M. and S. Nguyen, "An Application and Validation of Equilibrium Trip Assignment Models," *Transportation Science*, **10** (1976), 374–390.

[54] Forrester, J. W., *Industrial Dynamics*, Wiley: New York, 1961.

[55] Forrester, J. W., *Principles of Systems*, Cambridge, Mass.: Wright–Allen Press, 1968.

[56] Forrester, J. W., *Urban Dynamics*, Cambridge, Mass.: MIT Press, 1969.

[57] Frank, M. and P. Wolfe, "An Algorithm for Quadratic Programming," *Naval Research Logistics Quarterly*, **3** (1956), 95–110.

[58] Friesz, T. L., R. L. Tobin, T. E. Smith and P. T. Harker, "A Nonlinear Complementarity Formulation and Solution Procedure for the General Derived Demand Network Equilibrium Problem," *Journal of Regional Science*, **23** (1983), 337–359.

[59] Fujita, A., "Spatial Patterns of Urban Growth: Optimum and Market," *Journal of Urban Economics*, **3** (1976), 209–241.

[60] Fujita, A., "Existence and Uniqueness of Equilibrium and Optimal Land Use: Boundary Rent Curve Approach," *Journal of Regional Science and Urban Economics*, **15** (1985), 295–324.

[61] Fujita, M. and M. Kashiwadani, "The Spatial Growth of Tokyo: Theoretical and Empirical Analysis" in *Structural Economic Analysis and Planning in Time and Space*, ed. by W. Isard, A. E. Anderson, T. Puu and U. Schweizer, Amsterdam: North Holland, 1984.

[62] Fujita, M. and M. Kashiwadani, "Testing the Efficiency of Urban Spatial Growth: A Case Study of Tokyo," *Journal of Urban Economics*, (forthcoming).

[63] Fujita, M. and H. Ogawa, "Multiple Equilibria and Structural Transition of Nonmonocentric Urban Configurations," *Journal of Regional Science and Urban Economics*, **12** (1982), 161–196.

[64] Fullerton, D., J. B. Shoven and J. Whalley, "Replacing the U.S. Income Tax with a Progressive Consumption Tax: A Sequences General Equilibrium Approach," *Journal of Public Economics*, **20** (1983), 3–22.

[65] Glickman, N. J., "An Econometric Model of the Philadelphia Region," *Journal of Regional Science*, **11** (1971), 15–32.

[66] Glickman, *Econometric Analysis of Regional Systems: Explorations in Model Building and Policy Analysis*, New York: Academic Press, 1977.

[67] Goldner, W., *Projective Land Use Model* (PLUM), BATSC Technical Report 219, Bay Area Transportation Study Commission, Berkeley, California, 1968.

[68] Grieson, R. E., The Economics of Property Taxes: The Elasticity of Supply of Structures," *Journal of Urban Economics*, **1** (1974), 367–381.

[69] Hamilton, B. W., "Indivisibilities and Interplant Transportation Cost: Do They Cause Market Breakdown?," *Journal of Urban Economics*, **7** (1980), 31–41.

[70] Hamilton, B. and J. Whalley, "Tax Treatment of Housing in a Dynamic Sequenced General Equilibrium Model," Working Paper, No. 8425C, Department of Economics, The University of Western Ontario, 1984.

[71] Harris, B., "The City of the Future: The Problem of Optimal Design," *Papers of the Regional Science Association*, **19** (1967), 185–195.

[72] Harris, B., "Quantitative Models of Urban Development: Their Role in Metropolitan Policy Making" in *Issues in Urban Economics* ed. by H. Perloff and L. Wingo Jr., Baltimore: The Johns Hopkins University Press, 1968.

[73] Harris, B., J. Nathanson and L. Rosenburg, "Research on an Equilibrium Model of Metropolitan Housing and Locational Choice," Interim Report, University of Pennsylvania, Philadelphia, 1966.

[74] Harris, J. R. and M. P. Todaro, "Migration, Unemployment and Development: A Two-Sector Analysis," *American Economic Review*, **60** (1970), 126–142.

[75] Hartwick, J. M., "Price Sustainability of Location Assignments." *Journal of Urban Economics*, **1** (1984), 147–160.

[76] Hartwick, P. G. and J. M. Hartwick, "Efficient Resource Allocation in a

Multinucleated City with Intermediate Goods," *Quarterly Journal of Economics*, **88** (1974), 340–352.

[77] Hartwick, J., U. Schweizer and P. Varaiya, "Comparative Statics of a Residential Economy with Several Classes," *Journal of Economic Theory*, **13** (1976), 396–413.

[78] Heffley, D., "Efficient Spatial Allocation in the Quadratic Assignment Problem," *Journal of Urban Economics*, **3** (1976), 309–322.

[79] Heffley, D., "Competitive Equilibria and the Core of a Spatial Economy," *Journal of Regional Science*, **22** (1982), 423–440.

[80] Henderson, J. V., "The Sizes and Types of Cities," *American Economic Review*, **64** (1974), 640–656.

[81] Henderson, J. V., "Congestion and the Optimum City Size," *Journal of Urban Economics*, **2** (1975), 48–62.

[82] Henderson, J. V., "Systems of Cities in Closed and Open Economies," *Journal of Regional Science and Urban Economics*, **12** (1982), 325–350.

[83] Herbert, J. D. and B. H. Stevens, "A Model for the Distribution of Residential Activity in Urban Areas," *Journal of Regional Science*, **2** (1960), 21–36.

[84] Hill, D. M., "A Growth Allocation Model for the Boston Region," *Journal of the American Institute of Planners*, **31** (1965), 111–120.

[85] Hobson, P. A. R., "Local Tax Alternatives in a Two-Sector Urban Land Use Model: A Simulation Analysis," Department of Economics, The University of Western Ontario, 1985.

[86] Hopkins, L. D., "Optimum-Seeking Models for the Design of Suburban Land Use Plans," Ph.D. dissertation, Department of City and Regional Planning, University of Pennsylvania, Philadelphia, 1975.

[87] Horowitz, J. L., "The Stability of Stochastic Equilibrium in a Two-Link Transportation Network," *Transportation Research B*, **18** (1984), 13–28.

[88] Ingram, G. K., J. F. Kain and J. R. Ginn, *The Detroit Prototype of the NBER Urban Simulation Model*, New York: National Bureau of Economic Research, 1972.

[89] Isard, W., "Interregional and Regional Input–Output Analysis: A Model of a Space Economy," *Review of Economics and Statistics*, **33** (1951), 318–328.

[90] Isard, W., "Some Empirical Results and Problems of Regional Input–Output Analysis" in *Studies in the Structure of the American Economy* ed. by W. W. Leontieff *et al.*, New York: Oxford University Press, 1953.

[91] Isard, W. and T. Langford, "Impacts of Vietnam War Expenditures on the Philadelphia Economy," *Papers of the Regional Science Association*, **23** (1969), 217–265.

[92] Kain, J. F., W. C. Apgar, Jr. and J. R. Ginn, "Simulation of the Market Effects of Housing Allowances. Vol. I: Description of the NBER Urban Simulation Model," Harvard University, Cambridge, 1976.

[93] Kain, J. F., W. C. Apgar, Jr. and J. R. Ginn, "Simulation of the Market Effects of Housing Allowances. Vol. II: Baseline and Policy Simulations for Pittsburgh and Chicago," Harvard University, Cambridge, 1977.

[94] Kain, J. F., W. C. Apgar, Jr. and J. R. Ginn, "Revitalizing Central City Neighborhoods: An Evaluation of Concentrated Housing and Neighborhood Improvement Strategies," Harvard University, Cambridge, 1982.

[95] Kelley, A. C. and J. G. Williamson, "The Limits to Urban Growth:

Suggestions for Macromodeling Third World Economies," *Economic Development and Cultural Change*, **30** (1982), 595–624.

[96] Kelley, A. C. and J. G. Williamson, "A Computable General Equilibrium Model of Third World Urbanization and City Growth: Preliminary Comparative Statics," in *Modelling Growing Economies in Equilibrium and Disequilibrium*, ed. by A. C. Kelley, W. Sanderson and J. G. Williamson. Durham: Duke University Press, 1983.

[97] Kelley, A. C. and J. G. Williamson, *What Drives Third World City Growth? A Dynamic General Equilibrium Approach*. Princeton: Princeton University Press, 1984.

[98] Kim, T. J., "Alternative Transportation Modes in an Urban Land Use Model: A General Equilibrium Approach," *Journal of Urban Economics*, **6** (1979), 197–215.

[99] Kimbell, L. J. and G. W. Harrison, "General Equilibrium Analysis of Regional Fiscal Incidence," in *Applied General Equilibrium Analysis*, ed. by H. E. Scarf and J. B. Shoven. Cambridge: Cambridge University Press, 1984.

[100] King, A. T., "Computing General Equilibrium Prices for Spatial Economies," *The Review of Economics and Statistics*, **59** (1977), 340–350.

[101] King, A. T., "General Equilibrium with Externalities: A Computational Method and Urban Applications," *Journal of Urban Economics*, **7** (1980), 84–101.

[102] Klein, L. R., *Economic Fluctuations in the United States, 1921–1941*, New York: Wiley, 1950.

[103] Klein, L. R. and N. J. Glickman, "Econometric Model Building at Regional Level," *Journal of Regional Science and Urban Economics*, **7** (1977), 3–24.

[104] Knight, F. H., "Some Fallacies in the Interpretation of Social Cost," *Quarterly Journal of Economics*, **38** (1924), 582–606.

[105] Koopmans, T. C. and M. J. Beckmann, "Assignment Problems and the Location of Economic Activities," *Econometrica*, **1** (1957), 53–76.

[106] Kuhn, H. W. and J. G. MacKinnon, "The Sandwich Method for Finding Fixed Points," *Journal of Optimization Theory and Applications*, **17** (1979), 189–204.

[107] LeBlanc, L. J., "An Algorithm for the Discrete Network Design Problem," *Transportation Science*, **9** (1975), 183–199.

[108] LeBlanc, L. J. and D. E. Boyce, "A Bilevel Programming Algorithm For Exact Solution of the Network Design Problem with User-Optimal Flow," *Transportation Research B*, **20** (1986), 259–265.

[109] Leontieff, W., *The Structure of the American Economy 1919–1939*, New York: Oxford University Press, 1951.

[110] Lerman, S. R., "Location, Housing and Automobile Ownership and Mode to Work: A Joint Choice Model," *Transportation Research Record*, **610** (1977), 71–84.

[111] Lind, R. C., "Spatial Equilibrium, the Theory of Rents, and the Measurement of Benefits from Public Programs," *Quaterly Journal of Economics*, **87** (1973), 188–207.

[112] Livesey, D. A., "Optimum City Size: A Minimum Congestion Cost Approach," *Journal of Economic Theory*, **6** (1973), 144–161.

[113] Los, M., "Simultaneous Optimization of Land Use and Transportation in New Town Design," Ph.D. dissertation, Department of City and Regional Planning, University of Pennsylvania, Philadelphia, 1975.

[114] Los, M., "Optimal Network Problem without Congestion: Some Computational Results," Publication 40, Centre de Recherche sur les Transports, Universite de Montreal, Montreal, 1976.

[115] Lowry, I. S., "A Model of Metropolis," RM-4035-RC, Santa Monica; RAND Corporation.
[116] MacKinnon, J. G., "Urban General Equilibrium Models and Simplicial Search Algorithms," *Journal of Urban Economics*, 1 (1974), 161–183.
[117] MacKinnon, J. G., "A Technique for the Solution of Spatial Equilibrium Models," *Journal of Regional Science*, 16 (1976), 293–307.
[118] Marble, D. F. and W. L. Garrison, "Analysis of Transportation Networks: A Linear Programming Formulation," *Highway Research Board Proceedings*, 37 (1958), 1–17.
[119] Mayo, S., "Theory and Estimation in the Economics of Housing Demand," *Journal of Urban Economics*, 10 (1981), 95–116.
[120] McDonald, J. F. and H. W. Bowman, "Land Value Functions: A Reevaluation," *Journal of Urban Economics*, 6 (1979), 25–41.
[121] McFadden, D., "Conditional Logit Analysis and Qualitative Choice Behavior," in *Frontiers in Econometrics* ed. by P. Zarembka, New York: Academic Press, 1973.
[122] McFadden, D., "Modelling the Choice of Residential Location" in *Spatial Interaction Theory and Planning Models* ed. by A. Karlqvist *et al.* Amsterdam: North Holland, 1978.
[123] Miller, E. J. and S. R. Lerman, "Disaggregate Modeling of Retail Firms' Decisions: A Case Study of Clothing Retailers," *Environment and Planning A*, (1981).
[124] Mills, E. S., "Markets and Efficient Resource Allocation in Urban Areas," *Swedish Journal of Economics*, 74 (1972), 100–113.
[125] Mills, E. S., *Studies in the Structure of the Urban Economy*, Baltimore: Johns Hopkins Press, 1972.
[126] Mills, E. S., "Mathematical Models for Urban Planning" in *Urban and Social Economics in Market and Planned Economies*, ed. by A. Brown *et al.*, New York: Praeger, 1974.
[127] Mills, E. S., "Comments on Chapter Seven" in *Residential Location and Urban Housing Markets*, ed. by G. K. Ingram, Cambridge: Ballinger, 1977.
[128] Mills, E. S. and D. M. Deferranti, "Market Choices and Optimum City Size," *The American Economic Review*, 61 (1971), 340–345.
[129] Mills, E. S. and J. MacKinnon, "Notes on the New Urban Economics," *The Bell Journal of Economics and Management Science*, 4 (1973), 593–601.
[130] Moore, J. E., "Linearized, Optimally Configured Urban System Models: A Dynamic Mills Heritage Model with Replaceable Capital," Unpublished Ph.D. Dissertation, Stanford University, 1986.
[131] Moses, L. N., "Outputs and prices in Interindustry Models," *Papers of the Regional Science Association*, 32 (1974), 7–20.
[132] Muth, R. F., "The Derived Demand for Urban Residential Land," *Urban Studies*, 8 (1971), 243–254.
[133] Muth, R. F., "Numerical Solution of Urban Residential Land Use Models," *Journal of Urban Economics*, 2 (1975), 307–332.
[134] Ohls, J. C. and D. Pines, "Discontinuous Urban Development and Economic Efficiency," *Land Economics*, 51 (1975), 224–234.
[135] Pines, D., "Dynamic Aspects of Land Use Pattern in a Growing City" in *Mathematical Land Use Theory*, ed. G. J. Papageorgiou, Lexington: Heath, 1976.
[136] Pines, D. and E. Sadka, "Comparative Static Analysis of a Fully Closed City," *Journal of Urban Economics*, 20 (1986), 1–20.
[137] Preston, R. S., "The Wharton Annual and Industry Forecasting Model."

Studies in Quantitative Economics, No. 7 Philadelphia: University of Pennsylvania, Department of Economics, 1972.

[138] Putman, S. H., *Integrated Urban Models,* London: Pion Press, 1984.

[139] Quandt, R. E., "Models of Transportation and Optimal Network Construction," *Journal of Regional Science,* **2** (1962), 27–46.

[140] Quigley, J., "Housing Demand in the Short Run: An Analysis of Polytomous Choice" in *Explorations in Economic Research* ed. by S. D. Winter, **3** (1976), 76–102.

[141] Richter, D. K., "The Computation of Urban Land Use Equilibria," *Journal of Economic Theory,* **19** (1978), 1–27.

[142] Richter, D. K., "A Computational Approach to Resource Allocation in Spatial Urban Models," *Journal of Regional Science and Urban Economics,* **10** (1979), 17–42.

[143] Richter, D. K., "A Computational Approach to the Study of Neighborhood Effects in General Equilibrium Urban Land Use Models" in *The Economics of Neighborhood,* ed. by David, Segal, New York: Academic Press, 1979.

[144] Ridley, T. M., "An Investment Policy to Reduce the Travel Time in a Transportation Network," *Transportation Research,* **2** (1968), 409–424.

[145] Samuelson, P. A., "Spatial Price Equilibrium and Linear Programming," *American Economic Review,* **42** (1952), 283–303.

[146] Scarf, H., *The Computation of Economic Equilibria,* New Haven: Yale University Press, 1973.

[147] Scarf, H. and J. B. Shoven, *Applied General Equilibrium Analysis,* Cambridge: Cambridge University Press, 1984.

[148] Scott, A. J., "The Optimal Network Problem: Some Computational Procedures," *Transportation Research,* **3** (1969), 201–210.

[149] Shannon, C. and W. Weaver, *The Mathematical Theory of Communication,* Urbana: University of Illinois Press, 1949.

[150] Sheffi, Y., *Urban Transportation Networks: Equilibrium Analysis with Mathematical Programming Methods.* Englewood Cliffs: Prentice–Hall, 1985.

[151] Shelton, J. P., "The Cost of Renting versus Owning a Home," *Land Economics,* **1** (1968), 59–72.

[152] Shoven, J. B., and J. Whalley, "A General Equilibrium Calculation of the Effects of Differential Taxation on Capital in the U.S.," *Journal of Public Economics,* **1** (1972), 281–321.

[153] Shoven, J. B. and J. Whalley, "General Equilibrium with Taxes: A Computational Procedure and an Existence Proof," *Review of Economic Studies,* **40** (1973), 475–490.

[154] Shoven, J. B. and J. Whalley, "Equal Yield Tax Alternatives: General Equilibrium Computations," *Journal of Public Economics,* **3** (1977).

[155] Small, K. A. and H. S. Rosen, "Applied Welfare Economics with Discrete Choice Models," *Econometrica,* **49** (1981), 105–130.

[156] Solow, R. M., "Congestion Cost and the Use of Land for Streets," *Bell Journal of Economics and Management Science,* **4** (1973), 602–618.

[157] Solow, R. M. and W. S. Vickrey, "Land Use in a Long Narrow City," *Journal of Economic Theory,* **3** (1971), 430–447.

[158] Stairs, S., "Selecting an Optimal Traffic Network," *Journal of Transport Economics and Policy,* **2** (1967), 218–231.

[159] Strotz, R. H., "Urban Transportation Parables" in *The Public Economy of Urban Communities,* ed. by J. Margolis, Baltimore: Johns Hopkins, 1965.

[160] Struyk, R. J. and M. A. Turner, "Exploring the Effects of Racial Preferences

on Urban Housing Markets," *Journal of Urban Economics,* **19** (1986), 131–147.

[161] Sullivan, A. M., "A General Equilibrium Model with External Scale Economies in Production," *Journal of Urban Economics,* **13** (1983), 235–255.

[162] Sullivan, A. M., "The General Equilibrium Effects of Congestion Externalities," *Journal of Urban Economics,* **14** (1983), 80–104.

[163] Sullivan, A. M., "Second Best Policies for Congestion Externalities," *Journal of Urban Economics,* **14** (1983), 105–123.

[164] Sullivan, A. M., "The General Equilibrium Effects of the Industrial Property Tax: Incidence and Excess Burden," *Journal of Regional Science and Urban Economics,* **14** (1984), 547–564.

[165] Sullivan, A. M., "The General Equilibrium Effects of the Residential Property Tax: Incidence and Excess Burden," *Journal of Urban Economics,* **18** (1985), 235–250.

[166] Sullivan, A. M., "A General Equilibrium Model with Agglomerative Economies and Decentralized Employment," *Journal of Urban Economics,* **20** (1986), 55–74.

[167] Takayama, T. and G. C. Judge, *Spatial and Temporal Price Allocation Models,* New York: North-Holland, 1971.

[168] Theil, H., *Economics and Information Theory.* Chicago: Rand McNally. Amsterdam: North Holland, 1967.

[169] Turner, M. A. and R. J. Struyk, "Urban Housing in the 1980's: Markets and Policies," The Urban Institute, Washington, D.C., 1983.

[170] Vanski, J. and Ozanne, L., "Simulating the Housing Allowance Program in Green Bay and South Bend: A Comparison of the Urban Institute Housing Model and the Supply Experiment," Washington, D.C.: The Urban Institute, 1978.

[171] Vickrey, W. S., "Congestion Theory and Transport Investment," *American Economic Review Proceedings,* **59** (1969), 251–260.

[172] Wardrop, J. G., "Some Theoretical Aspects of Road Traffic Research," *Proceedings of the Institute of Civil Engineering, Part II,* **1** (1952), 325–378.

[173] Weibull, J. W., "A Dynamic Model of Trade Frictions and Disequilibrium in the Housing Market," *Scandinavian Journal of Economics,* **85** (1983), 373–392.

[174] Werner, C., "The Role of Topology and Geometry in Optimal Network Design," *Papers of the Regional Science Association,* **21** (1968), 173–189.

[175] Wheaton, W. C., "Income and Urban Location," Unpublished Ph.D., Dissertation, MIT, 1972.

[176] Wheaton, W. C., "A Comparative Static Analysis of Urban Spatial Structure," *Journal of Economic Theory,* **9** (1974), 223–237.

[177] Wheaton, W. C., "Linear Programming and Locational Equilibrium: The Herbert–Stevens Model Revisited," *Journal of Urban Economics,* **1** (1974), 278–287.

[178] Wheaton, W. C., "On the Optimal Distribution of Income Among Cities," *Journal of Urban Economics,* **3** (1976), 31–44.

[179] Wheaton, W. C., "Income and Urban Residence: An Analysis of Consumer Demand for Location," *American Economic Review,* **67** (1977), 620–631.

[180] Wheaton, W. C., "A Bid Rent Approach to Housing Demand," *Journal of Urban Economics,* **4** (1977), 200–217.

[181] Wheaton, W. C., "Urban Residential Growth Under Perfect Foresight," *Journal of Urban Economics,* **12** (1982), 1–21.

[182] Wheaton, W. C., "Urban Spatial Development with Durable but Replaceable Capital," *Journal of Urban Economics*, **12** (1982), 53–67.

[183] Wildasin, D. E., "Local Public Goods, Property Values, and Local Public Choice," *Journal of Urban Economics*, **6** (1979), 521–534.

[184] Williams, H. C. W. L., "On the Formation of Travel Demand Models and Economic Evaluation Measures of User Benefit," *Evnironment and Planning A*, **9** (1977), 285–344.

[185] Wilson, A. G., "A Statistical Theory of Spatial Distribution Models," *Transportation Research*, **1** (1967), 253–269.

INDEX

131

For Product Safety Concerns and Information please contact our EU
representative GPSR@taylorandfrancis.com Taylor & Francis Verlag GmbH,
Kaufingerstraße 24, 80331 München, Germany

Printed and bound by CPI Group (UK) Ltd, Croydon, CR0 4YY
08/05/2025
01864499-0002